PORTRAITS
OF THE NEW ARCHITECTURE
PHOTOGRAPHS BY RICHARD SCHULMAN

© 2004 Assouline Publishing, Inc.
All photographs © 2004 Richard Schulman, except for page 78.
Page 78 © 2004 Steve Double/Zaha Hadid Architects.

Assouline Publishing, Inc.
601 West 26th Street
18th floor
New York, NY 10001
USA
Tel.: 212 989-6810   Fax: 212 647-0005

www.assouline.com

ISBN: 2 84323 573 1

Color separation: Gravor (Switzerland)
Printing: Grafiche Milani (Italy)

Texts by Sarah Stein
Additional editing by Andrea Codrington

PORTRAITS
OF THE NEW ARCHITECTURE
PHOTOGRAPHS BY RICHARD SCHULMAN

Introduction by Paul Goldberger

Paul Goldberger [signature]

ASSOULINE

CONTENTS

Raimund Abraham 12

Tadao Ando 16

Arquitectonica 20

Shigeru Ban 24

Deborah Berke 28

Santiago Calatrava 32

David Childs 36

Henry Cobb 40

Elizabeth Diller and Ricardo Scofidio 44

Winka Dubbeldam 48

Peter Eisenman 52

Lord Foster 56

James Ingo Freed 60

Frank Gehry 64

Michael Graves 68

Charles Gwathmey 72

Zaha Hadid 76

Jacques Herzog and Pierre de Meuron 80

Steven Holl 84

Hans Hollein 88

Arata Isozaki 92

Toyo Ito 96

Philip Johnson 100

Rem Koolhaas 104

Ricardo Legorreta 108

Daniel Libeskind 112

Greg Lynn 116

Rodolfo Machado and Jorge Silvetti 120

Thom Mayne 124

Richard Meier 128

Eric Owen Moss 132

Enrique Norten 136

Jean Nouvel 140

William Pedersen 144

I.M. Pei 148

Cesar Pelli 152

Renzo Piano 156

Christian de Portzamparc 160

Antoine Predock 164

Wolf Prix 168

Lord Rogers 172

Lindy Roy 176

SANAA 180

SHoP 184

Robert A.M. Stern 188

Bernard Tschumi 192

Robert Venturi and Denise Scott Brown 196

Rafael Viñoly 200

Tod Williams and Billie Tsien 204

Peter Zumthor 208

FOREWORD

BY RICHARD SCHULMAN

Architects, one might say, have finally been unleashed. No longer constrained by repressive theory or narrow commercial concerns, architects are now free to be truly expressive, to confront the public psyche, to challenge the conventions of politics and taste. As a result, architecture has become not only an integral part of popular culture, but perhaps our greatest recognizable art form.

All of which at least partly explains why architects have become the new artistic superstars. In the past, the lot of most architects was to be treated as mere builders or as part of the background; now they are fawned over by the media and celebrated for their celebrity. We now take great pride in recognizing—and championing—various architects and their respective camps. In the past it was Picasso vs. Matisse; now it's Koolhaas vs. Gehry. A Koolhaas or Gehry unveiling is not (yet) on the order of a Hollywood premiere, but it is an event.

Of course, not all architects and architecture receive this level of adulation. And not every architect is deserving of what he or she has received. We are drawn to the bold, the shocking, the eccentric. Our eyes view the new architecture as part dazzling jewelry and part Cirque du Soleil eye-popping feat.

All of which has led to the inevitable criticism that there is now too much emphasis on the architect as personality, as rock star. Koolhaas himself refused to sit for an individual portrait, arguing that his group is just as important as he is. And, contrary to the notion of architect as solitary practitioner, Arata Isozaki told me that the collective nature of the new work reminds him of the architecture of classical antiquity "in its methods, and even in its attitude toward life."

Nevertheless, it's certainly well past time that architects in general receive their due. The idea for this book stemmed from a desire to celebrate architects, but to celebrate them for their talent, their visions, their brilliance—not their trendiness or dexterity at a press conference. The idea was also to explore the relationship between architects and their architecture, such as it exists.

Perhaps the hardest task was to narrow the list of architects to fifty. Today there are an inordinate number of great practitioners, great artists who push the limits, and great work. No doubt we left out more than a few who fulfill these criteria. What we have tried to construct is a cross section of architects—from different styles and generations—working at the end of the twentieth and the beginning of the twenty-first centuries. Then each of these architects was asked to choose which of their buildings most represents them (which, for the most part, I honored).

I like to think of a portrait, especially a portrait of a creative individual, as a journey, a journey into a person's space and mind. When you are photographing anyone, you wait for the perfect moment when a little bit of the self is exposed. But for artists, creators, the world expects something a bit more profound, a bit more intense. So what I try to do is use light to embrace my subject while at the same time creating openings within the light for the subject to (metaphorically) expand his or her self. It is quite a revelation to both listen to someone intimately explaining the significance of their work, and to watch their body language divulge still another variant of their emotions.

Similarly, there is a moment when light falls on a building in such away that my camera is able to capture its essence. But for me photographing architecture is as much about the happenstance discovery of a building as it is about the discovery of its personality. The fact is, the way we discover architecture is quite different from the way an architect would like us to. Yes, architects create architecture for basic ways of living, but they also create works to be looked at, to behold. Yet the way the average person perceives a building is by turning a corner from a crowded street and catching a glimmer from a reflection of light. The lure brings our attention to the attraction, and only then do we begin to come to terms with the design.

While on this journey, I was frequently asked: Can you tell anything about an architect from his work; can you tell anything about a work from its architect? To be honest, in all my scrutiny of a building I have never truly found the soul of the architect. But I have realized his or her concerns. The concerns are both pragmatic and part of a dramatic dance of ideas involving the past, present, and future. On the other hand, when I meet an architect, it is not necessarily the way he or she looks that reveals who or what he or she is about; it is the voice. It is the flow of information or thought that strikes a cord between the work and the self.

Of course, discovering architecture is an evolving process—a continual process of creative focus and analysis that allows each of us to be active participants. The ways that we engage architecture changes daily, and so do our pre-suppositions on how architecture should work and look. My hope is that this book is as much a reflection of this architectural moment as it is a tool, to help all of us hone our skills at discovery. For better or worse, as today's dance of ideas continues to bound from building to building, we are inevitably part of the conversation. If we don't want celebrity to count more than brilliance in this new era, we need to become as visually engaged as photographers at reading the new architecture—and the new architects.

INTRODUCTION

BY PAUL GOLDBERGER

Architects are not people who recede into the background. One would think that by being able to produce actual buildings—such conspicuous evidence of their creative force—they would not fear being overlooked. But it is rarely so. Few architects are content to let their work speak for them; most of them are determined to strut the stage themselves, along with their buildings. It is hardly true that ego in architecture is directly proportionate to talent—there are as many exceptions to that in this profession as in any other—but it is probably fair to say that there are relatively few architects who lack substantial egos. Almost all architects, having been conditioned to think large, see themselves not only as people of substance, but as people of power. They do, after all, shape things that are likely to outlast their own lives, and perhaps the lives of the next generation or two: unlike novelists and composers and painters, they do not have to be creating masterworks to assure that their work will be noticed after they are gone. Not the least of the paradoxes of the architecture profession is that the bad architects often have as big an impact on the landscape, and on the future, as the good ones.

Then again, if architects are not the most modest of people, it is not, of course, so easy to be an architect. You are part artist, part engineer, part businessman, part technocrat and manager, and part—perhaps more than part—salesman. If you act as if your work is only creative, then the realities of economics and politics and structural engineering will do you in, and if you act as if the mundane things matter more than the art of it all, then you will never be any good. It is a difficult life, and it is not for the faint of heart.

In Richard Schulman's portraits of architects, there are no faint-hearted figures. What is most astonishing about Schulman's work is how he manages to portray fifty of the most prominent architects practicing today as distinct personalities, each one different from all the others—to craft each portrait in a way that connects the image of the architect's persona to his or her work, and then to make of all of this a whole that is even more than the sum of its parts. That whole is a picture of the architect as cultural figure right now, a time when architects loom larger in the culture than ever before. Schulman presents the architect as celebrity, which indeed he is, but he does not kowtow to this phenomenon. He is able to honor the more prominent role architecture plays in the culture today while at the same time making it clear that he is aware of the expansive egos it yields, and is willing to tweak them gently, if not cut them down to size. This is not a book that will garner much favor among those who call for a more anonymous architecture. You cannot be an advocate of quiet, background architecture and see the world through Richard Schulman's lens. But neither is Schulman trying to bring us back to the crude and cartoonish view of the architect as the all-powerful figure misunderstood by lesser mortals, as Ayn Rand would have had us believe in *The Fountainhead*. The men and women in these pages are human, so much so that in some cases we perceive them as victims of the culture of celebrity more than as exploiters of it.

Schulman has captured the essence of architecture today: personality-driven, image-driven, but at the same time deeply engaging and exciting. We live in a moment of public passion for architecture, and every page of this book expresses this. This passion does not in itself mean that all the architecture we produce now is great or even good, but no matter; it is a start, and in any case it is impossible to claim that public engagement in the most public art is not in itself a good thing.

It is common to date the outpouring of public interest in architecture to the 1997 opening of Frank Gehry's remarkable Guggenheim Museum in Bilbao, Spain, but the reality is that Bilbao was as much an effect as a cause of the current sensibility. It represented a culmination of years of moving toward an increased willingness to see architecture as the basis for emotional experience—an increased willingness to celebrate expression and invention, not to mention the creative power and possibility inherent in new technologies. Gehry summed up all of these forces and put them together into a great work that, in and of itself, had the ability to push things even further, and as with all great art, made the world feel different from the way it had been before. But if Bilbao was not the sole begetter of what we might call the category of New High-Visibility Architecture With Emotional Impact, it is the symbolic beginning. It is as well the building that led an entire generation of non-architects to demand architecture that they would find emotionally and intellectually engaging.

And the more of this kind of architecture that gets built, the more the constituency for architecture grows. The age of architecture, if we can call it that, comes about in part because of architecture itself. Thus we have not only Gehry's Disney Hall in Los Angeles, an even greater building than Bilbao, but Tadao Ando's Museum of Modern Art in Fort Worth and Zaha Hadid's Contemporary Art Center in Cincinnati and Tod Williams and Billie Tsien's Folk Art Museum in New York and Raimund Abraham's Austrian Cultural Center in New York and Lord Foster's Swiss Re Tower in London and Bernard Tschumi's architecture school at Florida International University and Richard Meier's apartment towers on the Hudson River—and that is only the beginning. In an age in which the board of Lincoln Center hires Liz Diller and Ric Scofidio to redesign the cen-

9

ter's public plazas, when M.I.T. decides that it wants the calling card of its campus to be a series of conspicuous works of architecture by the likes of Frank Gehry and Steven Holl, and when the Port Authority of New York commissions Santiago Calatrava to design a new transit station for Lower Manhattan, there now seems to be a certain inevitability of institutions using architecture to put themselves on the map. Organizations that were once resistant to architecture now seem to consider having a notable building—a "signature building," to use that somewhat cloying phrase—to be an essential part of their public identity.

There are risks in all of this, of course, no matter how much you believe that the rising tide of architecture is more healthy than not. We are a society that is increasingly visual, and increasingly eager for the stimulation of a quick visual fix; wanting to be noticed at all costs means that we may find ourselves falling for the architectural equivalent of the tarted-up blonde rather than the brunette whose charms are subtle but more sustaining. Sometimes, as in Gehry's best work, instant allure does not preclude deeper, more long-lasting pleasures. But that is not always the case, and there are times when I suspect we will fall prey to the heady turn-on of a glamorous building and pass up something that may be a more profound work of architecture but is not nearly as exciting at first glance. And as we become increasingly accustomed to the idea that architecture is supposed to give us a kind of emotional high, are we not at risk of needing more and more of it, all the time, upping the ante as buildings that once would have excited us now become routine?

In the end, this may turn out to be the real way we pay a price for our new fixation—that we need each piece of architecture to be increasingly different, to make a louder and louder statement to attract our interest. (When every building is extraordinary, as Robert Venturi and Denise Scott Brown once said, then haven't they all become ordinary?) And while no one wants to return to the early modernist creed of functionalism above all (a creed that was honored more in the breach anyway), there are plenty of architects these days who seem to disdain practical concerns as so far beneath them as to be unworthy of any attention at all.

To say this is to risk spoiling the party, and a wonderful party it has been. I am most astonished at the extent to which the fascination for name-brand architecture has moved beyond its traditional realm of cultural institutions, universities, and houses for the rich, and into the sphere of commercial buildings. Real estate developers now want apartment towers by Calatrava, office buildings by Robert A.M. Stern, hotels by Jean Nouvel, and shopping centers by Daniel Libeskind. They have come to realize that architecture is a marketing tool in itself—that the name of the architect can have as much impact on the price of apartments as the number of closets.

Richard Schulman's portraits are the farthest thing imaginable from marketing tools, striking and memorable though they are. Schulman's style is mannered and far from casual, but it is deeply insightful. Whether it is Charles Gwathmey looking thoughtfully as he sits before the large grid of an old industrial window, or Santiago Calatrava gazing a bit too admiringly at his own sculptures, or Jean Nouvel looking like a character in a film noir, or Peter Eisenman affecting a casual disorder—Schulman has revealed the essence of each of these people. Diller and Scofidio come off as thoughtful and even understated; Norman Foster as a bit narcissistic as he stares at a model of his new Hearst tower now rising in New York; and Frank Gehry as strangely rabbinical. Rafael Viñoly is one of the few who manages to come off as even slightly playful, since Schulman has a tendency to encourage his subjects to take themselves rather too seriously. Yet one might think of the brilliant photograph of Henry Cobb, who is seen only in shadow behind a model of one of his towers, as far wittier. Schulman's wit also comes through in the image of Eric Owen Moss in reflection, and in the portrait of Renzo Piano as almost papal. And what are we to make of the picture of Christian de Portzamparc, who is presented as a tiny figure standing in the huge space atop his LVMH tower in Manhattan, looking out at the skyline? Is he inconsequential, or all powerful as the maker of the very space that appears to diminish him? It is difficult, on the other hand, not to be moved by the exquisite photograph of James Ingo Freed, who appears almost stoic, by the gentleness of Michael Graves, and by the warmth that Schulman has seemed to coax out of Venturi and Scott Brown.

In all of these images, there is a degree of ambiguity between the subjects' identity as architects and whatever other qualities they have as human beings. That is precisely as it should be. Schulman is asking us to think about the connections between architects and their work, but he is wise enough not to draw simple conclusions. Artists are never precisely like their work anyway: there is no easy correlation between an artist's character and the nature of the work he produces, and there is little to be gained in seeking one. Schulman, aside from being a portraitist, is an accomplished architectural photographer, and within the pages of this book are not only unique portraits of the architect-subjects, but images of many of their buildings that in some cases are among the finest that have been taken. These architectural photographs serve another purpose, too: they assure that, however bedazzling Schulman's portraits of these architects are, the architecture will still have the chance to speak for itself.

RAIMUND ABRAHAM

Born in Tyrol, in the Austrian Alps, Raimund Abraham spent his childhood among the horrors of World War II and came of age in the creative hothouse of postwar Vienna. Abraham's aesthetic—which combines radical modernism with an almost apocalyptic vision—was formed by these experiences. In 1964, after the suicide of a good friend, Abraham came to the United States for a two-week teaching position at the Rhode Island School of Design. Two weeks became seven years, and in 1971, Abraham moved from Providence to New York to teach at Cooper Union, where then director John Hejduk had created a forum for theory-driven architecture that did not concern itself with context and practicality, but was based on ideas about pure forms and geometries.

Proclaiming that he has too much respect for the act of building to build indiscriminately, Abraham has spent his career asking not what can be built but what *should* be built. Despite this seeming disdain and his reputation as an architectural mystic (created by his extraordinary body of drawings and poetic texts), Abraham's realized projects follow through on his promise. His design for the Austrian Cultural Forum in Midtown Manhattan, which was completed in 2002, is located on a twenty-five-foot-wide parcel of land, and bears a tilted zinc façade and terraced wedges that alternately suggest an Easter Island totem and the slicing blades of a guillotine—a visceral exploration of art and death on an otherwise ordinary city block.

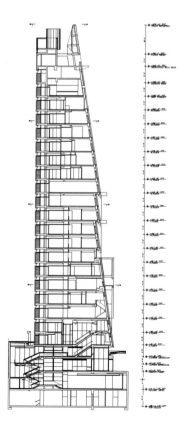 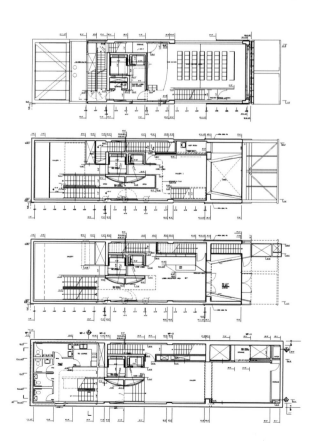

The Austrian Cultural Forum, New York.

The tower, rising autonomously between the existing walls of the adjacent structures, is defined by three syntactic elements, the Vertebra-Stair Tower, the Core-Structural Tower, and the Mask-Glass Tower, signifying the counter forces of gravity: Ascension, Support, and Suspension. Both the stair-tower as well as the curtain-wall strive for infinity—the stair-tower vertically, the curtain-wall diagonally. While the stair-tower is raising, the curtain-wall is falling by suspended sheets of glass and metal.

RAIMUND ABRAHAM,
ON THE AUSTRIAN CULTURAL FORUM

Raimund Abraham looking at Midtown Manhattan
from the top floor of the Austrian Cultural Forum, 2002.

TADAO ANDO

Tadao Ando is a self-trained architect. Although he never attended college, Ando spent his youth traveling extensively and visiting the studios of the architects he admired, including Alvar Aalto, Le Corbusier, and Louis Kahn. After returning to Osaka, Ando began designing small residences, and the rest is architectural history.

Ando's buildings are calm and serene, although they occasionally exhibit a severity that is tempered by a high degree of refinement. Some of Ando's most representative works are those he designed as places of worship. The small Church of the Light in Osaka is probably his best-known building in Japan. An oblong concrete box, the interior of the church slopes down toward the altar. Vertical and horizontal slits perforate the rear wall, creating a cross of natural light behind the altar. Simple and direct, the Church of the Light achieves a sense of awe akin to that of the great medieval cathedrals. His work on museum projects, including the 2002 Modern Art Museum of Fort Worth and the 2001 Pulitzer Foundation for the Arts, brings this sense of the sublime to secular culture.

Although his material of choice is reinforced concrete, and most of his buildings have few if any windows, Ando practices an architecture of light and air that provides a place of rest for the individual, whether that entails being isolated with works of art at the stark, curvilinear Naoshima Contemporary Art Museum in Okayama, Japan, or in the sloping confines of his Japanese Pavilion at the Seville Expo.

The museum is conceived as "An Arbor for Art," indicating that the whole of this extensive site is conceived of as an environment for the unhurried appreciation of art The intention is to provide a truly open museum, one that will serve as refreshing oasis in the midst of the severe local climate and an arbor of peace to stimulate the spirit of creativity.

**TADAO ANDO,
ON THE MODERN ART MUSEUM OF FORT WORTH**

Tadao Ando in the photographer's studio, 2003.

The Modern Art Museum of Fort Worth, Fort Worth, Texas.

Bernardo Fort-Brescia
and Laurinda Spear at
their home in Miami, 2003.

ARQUITECTONICA

Arquitectonica is based in Miami. This simple fact sums up the design philosophy of the firm headed by Bernardo Fort-Brescia and Laurinda Spear. While their fellow students at Harvard and Columbia were heading to New York and Chicago to begin their professional careers, the pair went to Miami—the city of Morris Lapidus and Little Havana—and became the first firm of the baby-boom generation to build large-scale commissions. The studio's first major work—the Spear House, designed with Rem Koolhaas in 1977 for Laurinda Spear's parents—was one of the most photographed buildings of the late 20th century; and the Atlantis condominium complex's "sky court" famously punctuated the credits of that 1980s icon, "Miami Vice."

Using brightly colored geometric forms, Fort-Brescia and Spear taught modernism the mambo, and in the process created a new visual identity for Miami. In 2003, Arquitectonica brought its lively brand of modernism north with the Westin New York hotel on the most famous spot in all of Manhattan, 42nd Street. With its over-the-top façade and colors, the Westin captures the essence of Times Square's unholy alliance of eroticism and consumerism while adding a Latin rhythm to America's most dynamic city.

The Westin New York is our first tall building in New York City. Our challenge was to design a skyscraper that fit the character of Times Square as defined by the guidelines prepared by Robert A.M. Stern in his urban design study for the neighborhood.

BERNARDO FORT-BRESCIA AND LAURINDA SPEAR, ON THE WESTIN NEW YORK

Westin New York
Times Square

SHIGERU BAN

In an era when architects have competed for increasingly grand and lucrative commissions using high-tech materials, Shigeru Ban has been building innovative, low-cost shelters for refugees around the world using nothing more than paper and the belief that architectural beauty should be accessible to even the poorest.

Born in Tokyo in 1957, Ban studied architecture at Southern California Institute of Architecture and at Cooper Union, where he received his bachelor of architecture in 1984. Ban's early work merged Western modernism with traditional Japanese elements and an ever-innovative use of basic materials. His 1995 Curtain Wall House recast Le Corbusier and Mies van der Rohe's nonstructural glass façades in white fabric to stunning effect. And his 1997 Wall-less House inverted the form of Cooper director John Hejduk's Wall House to create an open, flexible space. In 1997, Ban's Hangei Forest apartment house contrived to preserve a preexisting grove of trees while still remaining under budget.

But Ban has gained the most recognition for his work as consultant to the United Nations High Commissioner for Refugees, and as founder of the Volunteer Architects' Network, which helps communities in crisis. Ban is, literally, a cardboard architect, using low-cost materials to offer relief to displaced people. Although Ban used cardboard early in his career for exhibition designs, he really started thinking about it as a viable construction material after the devastating 1995 Kobe earthquake. It was then that he created an impromptu community hall and houses for those left homeless by the disaster out of thick cardboard tubes. Ban's paper-log houses included functioning doors and windows that rested on foundations made from beer crates.

In Rwanda and Turkey, Ban has used paper tubes as a structural alternative to aluminum frames, believing that emergency shelters need to be beautiful in order to aid in the psychological healing of the victims. But Ban's low-born material has also had its high-style manifestations: his Expo 2000 pavilion in Hanover was completely recycled when the fair closed.

A random grouping of twenty-seven large trees remained on this land in a quiet residential district in Tokyo. What was required was to build an apartment house without cutting down any of the existing trees, while, at the same time, staying within a restricted budget.

SHIGERU BAN, ON THE HANGEI FOREST

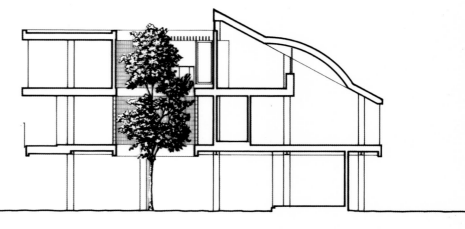

The Hangei Forest, Tokyo.

Shigeru Ban
in Shibuya-ku, Tokyo, 2003.

DEBORAH BERKE

After studying architecture at the Rhode Island School of Design and launching her eponymous studio in 1982, Deborah Berke first became known through a series of nineteen commercial and residential buildings she designed in the late 1980s for the "new urbanist" community of Seaside, Florida. The buildings emphasized a stripped-down austerity that stood in contrast to much of the architecture of the decade. In 1997, Berke, along with Steven Harris, co-authored *Architecture of the Everyday*, a book that urged architects to move beyond catchy labels and abstract theory in order to focus on human needs and recognize the power of the ordinary.

Yet despite her down-to-earth ethos, Berke's architectural prominence owes much to the fashion world, which has brought her numerous commissions. The Industria Superstudio—a 1930s-era New York garage that Berke converted into a place for parties and photo shoots—contrasts the rough, industrial quality of the original space with an understated crispness. And in a similar conversion, Berke transformed a drab 57th Street office into a penthouse aerie for creative director Fabien Baron's boutique ad agency.

Strongly influenced by the ordinary and displaying a keen awareness of the lived uses of her designs, Berke has created a pragmatic, minimal architecture. With projects such as the 2001 Yale School of Art and New Theater—where she expanded and restored an abandoned Jewish community center—and her design for the Hope Library in Columbus, Indiana, Berke's work strives for aesthetic accessibility and contextual sensitivity.

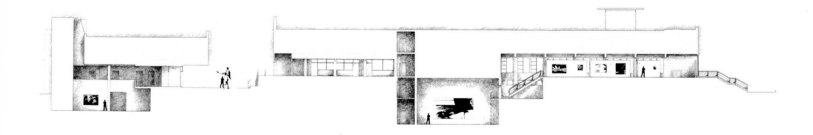

Deborah Berke in her Manhattan studio, 2004.

The Yale School of Art building proposes quasi-anonymity in lieu of "signature architecture." The hand of the architect is visible only with careful scrutiny. The School of Art's architecture functions in the background to what is most important: providing clean, elegant spaces for the solitude of making art and for the community formed through the teaching of the making of art.

DEBORAH BERKE, ON THE YALE SCHOOL OF ART

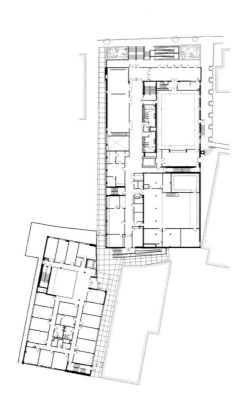

The Yale School of Art,
New Haven, Connecticut.

SANTIAGO CALATRAVA

Born to an aristocratic family in Valencia, Spain, Santiago Calatrava began his formal instruction in drawing and painting at the Arts and Crafts School when he was 8-years-old. After completing his architecture studies in Valencia, he decided to pursue postgraduate studies in civil engineering at the Federal Institute of Technology in Zurich, where he received his Ph.D. in 1979. Four years later, Calatrava opened his own studio in that city.

Since then, Calatrava has developed a worldwide reputation for designing aerodynamic structures that are both ethereal and solid and seem lifted into the air as if by sails. Not surprisingly, most of his important projects are for places of passage like bridges and terminals. Calatrava's many bridge designs include footbridges in Venice and Dublin, as well as the 1,544-foot-long Pont de L'Europe in Orléans, the 700-foot-long Alamillo bridge in Seville, the Campo Volantin footbridge in Bilbao, and the Turtle Bay Sundial Bridge in Sacramento. His terminals include the Lyon Airport Station, the Sondica Airport in Bilbao, the Oriente railway station in Lisbon, and the wing-like PATH Terminal, which will be built at the foot of the new World Trade Center in New York. One of Calatrava's boldest designs, however, is the Quadracci Pavilion for the Milwaukee Art Museum. The pavilion graces the lakeshore with a sculptural presence that complements the complex's original buildings by Eero Saarinen and David Kahler.

I wanted to do something that would feel like an addition to the lakefront, more than an addition to the two existing buildings. It would be interesting to make a bridge from the museum into the city, like an arm that reaches out and touches the city; and it would be interesting to create canopies on each side, like another arm, to emphasize the topography; and it would be interesting to add a brise soleil that can open and close like a bird's wings.

SANTIAGO CALATRAVA, ON THE QUADRACCI PAVILION

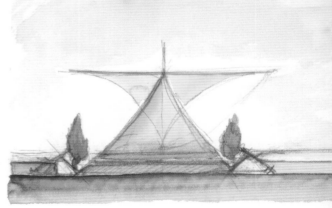

Santiago Calatrava
at his home in Manhattan, 2004.

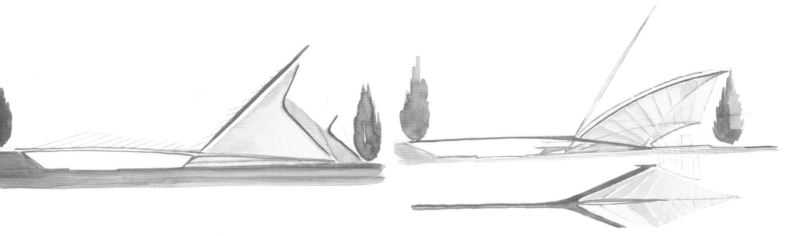

The Quadracci Pavilion, Milwaukee Art Museum,
Milwaukee, Wisconsin.

David Childs in the lobby of the Bear Stearns Headquarters
in Midtown Manhattan, 2002.

DAVID CHILDS

Four years after completing his architecture studies at Yale, David Childs joined the Washington, D.C., office of Skidmore, Owings & Merrill. A short four years later, President Ford named him chairman of the National Capital Planning Commission. During Childs' Washington years, he created the building plan and landscape design for the Great Mall and Constitution Gardens, the expansion of the Dulles Airport main terminal, and the headquarters for National Geographic.

In 1984, Childs moved to SOM's New York office, where he established a reputation for designing skyscrapers such as Bertelsmann Tower, the Bear Stearns Headquarters, the Times Square Tower, and the Time Warner Center at Columbus Circle, which was completed in 2003. All of which set the stage for his most important commission, and what will certainly be the most visible building of the early twenty-first century: the Freedom Tower, a 1,776-foot-tall skyscraper for the World Trade Center site to be built in collaboration with Daniel Libeskind.

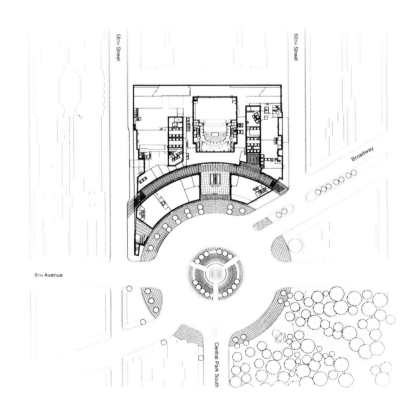

The Time Warner Center, perhaps to a greater extent than any other modern American building, exemplifies the concept of a city within a building, versus a building within a city. The building's form and imagery is derived from the very essence of the urban context from which it emanates—the Manhattan grid.

DAVID CHILDS, ON THE TIME WARNER CENTER

The Time Warner Center, New York.

HENRY COBB

Henry Cobb has a penchant for modernist angular geometry, which might seem strange coming from a native Bostonian whose background includes the hale and hearty traditions of Exeter and Harvard. But as one of the founding principals of Pei Cobb Freed & Partners, he has contributed actively to the transformation of his hometown skyline since the firm's formation in 1955.

In 1976, Cobb created what is perhaps his best-known building, the John Hancock Tower—a 2-million-square-foot glass skyscraper that has dominated the Boston skyline since its completion. The following decade saw the completion of two of the firm's skyscrapers in Dallas—the 1983 ARCO Tower and the 1986 Fountain Place, which includes a surrounding water garden that was designed by the landscape architect Dan Kiley. More recently, Cobb has designed the World Trade Center and Grand Marina Hotel in Barcelona, the Tour EDF in Paris, and the National Constitution Center in Philadelphia.

Other award-winning projects by Cobb include the Charles Shipman Payson Building, an addition to the Portland Museum of Art in Maine in 1983, and the College-Conservatory of Music in Cincinnati in 1999. His 1998 design of the John Joseph Moakley United States Courthouse in Boston mediates the bustling public space of Fan Pier outside with the cloistered public space of the courtyard inside through a number of interventions, including a rotunda lined with Ellsworth Kelly paintings. From 1980 to 1985 he served as studio professor and chairman of the department of architecture at the Harvard Graduate School of Design, and in 1992 he was architect in residence at the American Academy in Rome, where he also served as a trustee from 1972 to 1990.

*The decision to build a new United States Courthouse on this privileged
and highly visible site was perforce also a command to give voice, through architecture,
to those aspirations and beliefs that underlie the American system of jurisprudence.*

HENRY COBB, ON THE JOHN JOSEPH MOAKLEY UNITED STATES COURTHOUSE

Henry Cobb, photographed at his office, 2002.

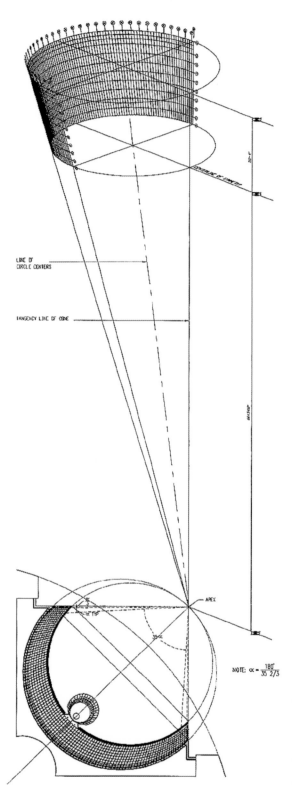

The John Joseph Moakley United States Courthouse, Boston.

ELIZABETH DILLER
RICARDO SCOFIDIO

You could call Elizabeth Diller and Ricardo Scofidio paper architects who conceive of innovative projects that ultimately never get built. But that would depend on your definition of the word "built." Indeed, what the pair has done—through site-specific art works, multimedia theater, and digital manipulations—is expand the definition of architecture. Ever since opening a studio in 1979, the husband-and-wife team has questioned the ways in which man-made environments affect public interactions, as well as how the immaterial can be made physical through shifts in perception.

Diller + Scofidio's early work took its cue from installation and performance art as much as from traditional architectural practice. In 1981, for example, the partners assembled 2,500 orange safety cones in Columbus Circle in an effort to demonstrate traffic patterns. And their now-iconic 1989 Slow House—an unbuilt seaside retreat on Long Island for a Japanese art investor—questioned what it meant to "have a view" by manipulating the way the client would enter the site.

The team's more recent work fluctuates between the poetic and the paranoid. The Blur Building, a pavilion built on Lake Neuchâtel for Expo 2002, consists of a steel structure covered with thousands of nozzles that generate obscuring clouds of mist. And in the Brasserie restaurant, completed in 2000, in Mies van der Rohe's Manhattan Seagram Building, fifteen monitors positioned over the bar record each arrival.

Having recently won the MacArthur Foundation's "genius" award, Diller + Scofidio have been given a number of high-visibility commissions, including the redesign of public spaces in and around Lincoln Center, the design of new buildings for the Institute of Contemporary Art in Boston, and the new Museum of Art & Technology for Eyebeam Atelier in New York.

The Brasserie, Seagram Building, New York.

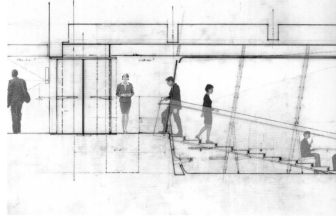

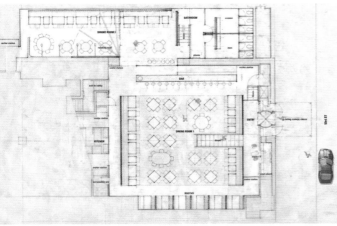

The prospect of redesigning one of New York's legendary restaurants in one of the world's most distinguished modernist buildings was as inviting as it was daunting. The architecture of the new restaurant respectfully challenges many of the tenets of modernism.

ELIZABETH DILLER AND RICARDO SCOFIDIO, ON THE BRASSERIE

Elizabeth Diller and Ricardo Scofidio,
in their Manhattan studio, 2002.

WINKA DUBBELDAM

Winka Dubbeldam thinks that the façade of a building is like a raincoat—a climatological device, and nothing more. Despite this opinion, Dubbeldam has gone a long way in transforming the aesthetics of this vestigial architectural detail. It is the main feature of her new eleven-story apartment building in downtown New York, appearing as a wave-like glass curtain wall custom-designed by a 3-D computer model. It is a striking point of distinction when compared to the neighborhood's otherwise poker-faced buildings.

The Dutch-born architect is fascinated by the challenges of creating sculptural design using computers. Her studio, Archi-Tectonics, which she founded in 1994 two years after completing Columbia's graduate architecture program is conceived as a laboratory where research and development are paramount and the computer is used as an ideation and inspirational tool; Archi-Tectonics has designed a number of residential projects in both urban and rural contexts, including the 2002 Gipsy Trail residence, situated on the edge of the Croton Reservoir and angled for maximum light and views. Having worked for renowned New York architects Bernard Tschumi and Peter Eisenman, Dubbeldam has evolved a studio strategy that combines the theoretical underpinnings of her Columbia education with the pragmatic matters of built construction.

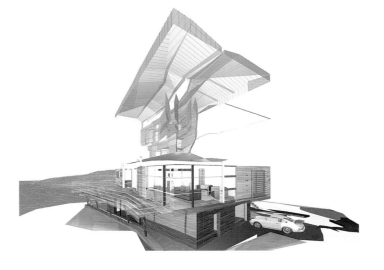

Winka Dubbeldam in her Manhattan studio, 2002.

The Gipsy Trail residence, Kent, New York.

At Croton Reservoir in upstate New York, the hills tumble right into the lake. Simultaneously soft and hard, rolling and jagged, the lakefront alternates green patches with craggy, rock formations. And built into this landscape of leaf and rock and water is a house—the Gipsy Trail residence.

WINKA DUBBELDAM, ON THE GIPSY TRAIL RESIDENCE

PETER EISENMAN

Peter Eisenman has become part of the architecture establishment almost despite himself. He has made a career of setting himself apart from mainstream architecture, founding the countercultural Institute for Architecture and Urban Studies in 1967, and developing projects that were inspired by the language theories of Noam Chomsky and the deconstructionism of Jacques Derrida. In recent years, Eisenman has surreptitiously entered the mainstream with the completion of several major commissions and the widespread adoption of his critical vocabulary by graduate students throughout the world.

Eisenman has long been a part of the architectural academy, first as a student at Cornell, Columbia, and Cambridge universities, then as a professor at Princeton, Yale, Harvard, and Ohio State. But Eisenman's 1991 design for the Wexner Center for the Arts, in Columbus, Ohio, marked his unofficial transition from esoteric academe to practicing builder. Drawing its architectural vocabulary from Derrida's deconstructionist theories of language and the demise of authorship, the Wexner is based on a perverse sort of contextualism. Instead of using the façade of the museum to blend into the surrounding area, Eisenman took the site's context—two preexisting Cartesian grids, on which the city of Columbus and the Ohio State University are plotted, and a demolished armory that had been on the site—and created something entirely new but inextricably bound to its place.

Since founding his own firm in 1980, Eisenman has come to specialize in projects that have inherent complexities, whether in terms of location, history, or budgetary constraints. Since German reunification, Eisenman has worked on several projects in Berlin, including social housing at Checkpoint Charlie, along the site of the former Wall, and a memorial to the murdered Jews of Europe. In addition to this historically resonant work, Eisenman has taken on the emphatically American—and lighthearted—task of designing a stadium for the Arizona Cardinals foot-ball team.

Peter Eisenman in his Manhattan office, 2001.

Instead of expressing its function as a shelter for art, the Wexner Center acts as a symbol of art as process and idea, of the ever-changing nature of art and society. In the great nineteenth-century tradition, the center is a fusion of landscape and the language of building.

PETER EISENMAN, ON THE WEXNER CENTER

The Wexner Center for the Arts,
Ohio State University, Columbus.

LORD FOSTER

Born into a working-class family in a suburb of Manchester in 1935, Norman Foster was somewhat of an unlikely candidate to become an award-winning architect—much less the recipient of lifetime peerage by Queen Elizabeth. But after graduating from high school and spending a few years in the Royal Air Force, Foster studied architecture at the University of Manchester and then at Yale, where he earned his master's degree and met fellow student Richard Rogers. In 1963, the two architects founded Team 4 and, three years later, Foster Associates, with Foster's wife, Wendy.

Foster's most formidable early influence was Buckminster Fuller, with whom he worked on a number of collaborations that lasted until Fuller's death in 1983. The American visionary had a profound influence on Foster's later designs—including the 2004 tower he created for Swiss Re, in London, based on ideas he first explored with Fuller while designing the early 1970s Climatroffice—and on his commitment to creating environmentally conscious buildings. Foster created an energy-efficient plan for London's Stansted Airport by turning the conventions of airport design inside out. Placing the infrastructure below the concourse, he constructed a glass casing around the terminal that allowed natural light to enter the building. The success of Stansted led to his commission to build Chek Lap Kok, the world's largest airport, in Hong Kong.

Foster's elegant structures are most striking when integrated into preexisting historical buildings—another kind of conservation altogether. Foster's trademark glass dome for the rebuilt Reichstag, in Berlin, expresses the German government's commitment to transparency, while his similarly grand glass and steel roof for the Great Court at the British Museum creates a distinct sense of openness in an otherwise cloistered space.

It is an instantly recognizable addition to London's skyline and was designed as the capital's first ecological skyscraper. The environmental strategy uses natural ventilation and daylight as part of a controlled climate—to improve the quality of the workplace and reduce energy and carbon emissions. Visually, it is bold but gentle—creating more public space at the base for terraces, outdoor cafés, and shopping. As I look across the River Thames from our home on the lower skyline of the city, I can see it from a distance glinting in the sunlight.

NORMAN FOSTER, ON THE SWISS RE TOWER

Norman Foster, looking at his model for the Hearst Building, within the building itself, 2002.

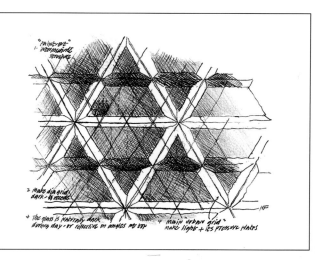

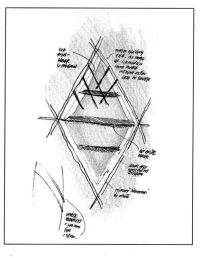

The Swiss Re tower, London.

James Ingo Freed in his Lower Manhattan office, 2002.

JAMES INGO FREED

As a student at the Illinois Institute of Technology, James Ingo Freed was greatly influenced by the stark minimalism of the school's legendary director, Ludwig Mies van der Rohe. After graduation, Freed was invited by the German master to work in New York on the Seagram Building, but left after a year to join I.M. Pei's fledgling firm. For the next two decades, Freed produced works for Pei such as the Jacob Javits Center in New York in 1986 and the First Bank Place tower in 1992—both of which were indebted to his early experience and adhered to a modernism rooted in functionalism and minimalism. Freed found himself, however, increasingly dissatisfied with the products of the Internationalist aesthetic. The ubiquity of anonymous glass boxes that cropped up in every city during the 1960s and '70s turned Freed toward architecture that had more of a relationship to history and urban context.

A definitive break with modernist austerity came in 1993 with Freed's commission for the United States Holocaust Museum. Designing a work so fundamentally linked with history and place led Freed on an intimate journey of remembrance. But an immersion in Holocaust literature and images was not enough to inspire Freed, who had fled from Nazi Germany at the age of nine, and recalls having spent *Kristallnacht* riding streetcars with his father, their faces hidden behind anti-Semitic newspapers. Freed traveled with museum founding director Arthur Rosenblatt to former concentration camps in Germany and Poland, which forced him to confront his own memories and prompted him to look at how architecture was put to use in the design of the camps.

Using only architecture as a means for engaging an unknowing public makes for a difficult problem. The attack on this problem lies within the realm of a tectonic development and in the planar, superimposition of spaces within a central exterior-internal orbit. This, of course, moves the exterior definition of the building inside, where the combination establishing a new reality takes place.

JAMES INGO FREED,
ON THE UNITED STATES HOLOCAUST MUSEUM

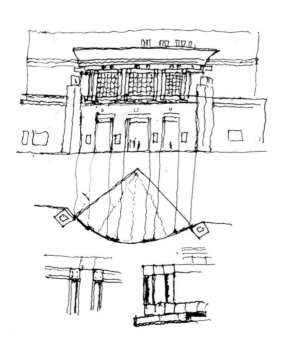

The United States Holocaust Museum,
Washington, D.C.

FRANK GEHRY

The first piece of art to be installed in Frank Gehry's Guggenheim Museum Bilbao was Richard Serra's *Snake*—a fitting gesture for an architect whose work veers as much towards sculpture as Serra's does towards architecture. Not surprisingly, the Toronto-born architect has predicated his entire career on blurring the line between art and architecture. Gehry's first notable project—the 1978 remodeling of his own home in Santa Monica, California—employed a mix of plywood, chain-link fence, galvanized zinc, and cinder block arranged in a mass of riotous form that employed a wholly new architectural vocabulary of "unfinished" materials.

In the years that followed, Gehry designed emphatically sculptural buildings like the Venice, California, office of advertising firm Chiat/Day, which featured an entrance created by sculptors Claes Oldenburg and Coosje van Bruggen in the form of outsize binoculars. Gehry also began designing furniture—an activity he initially used to work out the complex manipulation of materials at a low cost and small scale—which resulted in the now-legendary Easy Edges line of corrugated cardboard chairs and tables.

But Gehry's first world-class building was his voluptuous, titanium-clad Guggenheim Museum Bilbao, which coined a phrase indicating the phenomenon of urban renewal through architecture: "the Bilbao effect." Other recent projects have included the 2004 Walt Disney Concert Hall—the first large-scale public project Gehry has built in his hometown of Los Angeles—and the 2000 Experience Music Project in Seattle. With their swooping walls and gleaming façades, Gehry's work reasserts the power of the individual imagination in the face of postmodernism's denial of the author—a factor that played into his being awarded the much-coveted Pritzker Architecture Prize, as well as the National Medal of Arts and the Friedrich Kiesler Prize.

Frank Gehry in his Los Angeles studio, 1995.

The Walt Disney Concert Hall was designed from the inside out. We began with the design of the hall itself. Every decision was guided by the goal of creating the best possible acoustics for symphonic performances. We designed the outside of the building in response to the inside, but also in response to the surroundings. Our goal was to make the building casual, accessible, and inviting.

FRANK GEHRY, ON THE WALT DISNEY CONCERT HALL

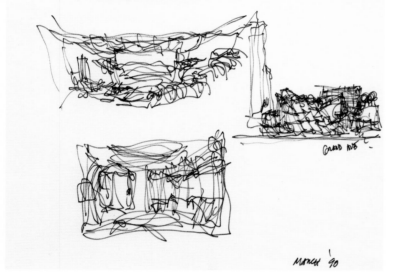

The Walt Disney Concert Hall, Los Angeles.

MICHAEL GRAVES

From his modest beginnings as a designer of small house additions and a painter of murals, Michael Graves has become one of the most influential designers in America. A native of Indianapolis, Graves received his architectural training at the University of Cincinnati and at Harvard, and won the Rome Prize in 1960 to study at the American Academy.

It was during his time in Rome that Graves hit upon the idea that architectural elements like roofs, windows, and columns were the nouns and verbs of visual language. Consequently, Graves has become known for a recombinant eclecticism that is punctuated equally by classical allusion and wit. Since 1964, the Princeton-based Michael Graves & Associates has undertaken a variety of architectural projects that include every category of building imaginable. Recent commissions include the renovation of the 10,000-square-meter historic Shanghai Bund Art Center in China, which features two atria and a grand staircase that unify the complex's original 1916 structures. Graves' renowned work for Disney includes the Dolphin hotel for Disney World and his 1986 Team Disney Building in Burbank, which famously incorporates the iconic Seven Dwarves on a massive scale to hold up the structure's gable. A 2000 residential building in Manhattan's Murray Hill has propelled Michael Graves to the New York skyline.

Most recently, Graves has become equally well known as a product designer. His 1985 design for an Alessi teapot with a whistling spout that looks like a bird elevated Graves to stardom; more than half a million have been sold. In the last 20 years, his studio has designed more than 1,000 consumer products, ranging from wood-handled feather dusters and dartboards to watches, textiles, bathroom fixtures, and furniture. The retail chain Target has released a Michael Graves line that includes a pared-down version of his Alessi teapot, as well as three models for outbuildings that can be built as freestanding structures or attached to an existing house.

Michael Graves at his home in Princeton, New Jersey, 1999.

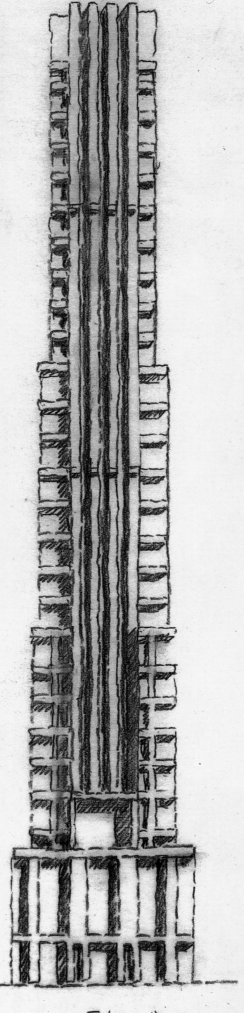

*In designing 425 Fifth Avenue,
we aspired to create a sense
of domesticity consistent with
the models of grand New York
City apartment buildings, such
as the San Remo, the Dakota,
and other romantically
named residential buildings
from the past century.*

MICHAEL GRAVES, ON 425 FIFTH AVENUE

425 Fifth Av.
'01

425 Fifth Avenue, New York.

CHARLES GWATHMEY

In 1965, Charles Gwathmey built his parents a house in Amagansett, New York, that firmly established the 27-year-old architect as one of his generation's most original talents. Cool and simple, the house espoused a rejection of the social concerns of the 1960s in favor of an exploration of the aesthetics of pure form. Looking back to the great modernist projects of Le Corbusier, Gwathmey, along with the rest of the "New York Five"—Peter Eisenman, Michael Graves, John Hejduk, and Richard Meier—extracted not the Swiss master's utopian dream, but rather his aesthetic of pure, elegant abstraction.

After the stunning success of the house in Amagansett, Gwathmey teamed up with partner Robert Siegel in 1968 and started building elegant, modernist houses that became fashionable on Long Island's South Shore and in the area surrounding L.A. His renowned 1999 residence in Malibu stands as one of his hallmarks—a pristine white presence that integrates the surrounding landscape through interlocking volumes.

Gwathmey has not confined himself to the world of residential architecture. His design for the expansion of Frank Lloyd Wright's landmark Guggenheim Museum in New York proved that he could adapt a beloved building with the appropriate degree of reverence while still remaining true to his own artistic vision. Having already completed major works in such fields as educational buildings, cultural complexes, and athletic facilities, Gwathmey, Siegel & Associates is currently working on projects as diverse as a library for Middlebury College, the Jewish Children's Museum in Brooklyn, and a waterfront W Hotel in Hoboken, New Jersey.

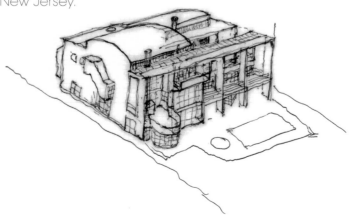

Charles Gwathmey in his studio, 2001.

We've done over thirty-five houses and investigated many formal arrangements. The Malibu residence is a great summary of the investigation of the pavilion and Le Corbusier's double-height prototype, and the combination makes the house an enriched spatial experience.

CHARLES GWATHMEY, ON THE MALIBU RESIDENCE

Malibu residence, Malibu, California.

ZAHA HADID

For close to twenty years, London-based architect Zaha Hadid was more famous for the high-profile competitions she won through a combination of rigorous research and artful renderings than for the structures she actually built. Hadid was born into an affluent Baghdad family during the period between the withdrawal of British power and the rise of the Baath party. The architect's father was a prominent industrialist and member of the National Democratic party, and the young Hadid felt there were no limits on what a girl might aspire to be—and she wanted to be an architect.

Arriving at London's Architectural Association in 1972, by way of a Swiss boarding school and the American University in Beirut, Hadid and her contemporaries were encouraged to forget about the practicalities of built work and instead practice an architecture based on conjecture and plausibility, often supported by reams of theory. Her experience at the AA led to a longtime working partnership with the Dutch architect and theorist Rem Koolhaas, with whom she collaborated at his Office for Metropolitan Architecture before coming to the United States for a period of teaching at Harvard and Yale.

Hadid's status as the ultimate paper architect and visionary conceptualist was not due to a desire to remain within the world of theory, but rather the result of a series of frustrations. First there was a winning design for the Peak, a leisure complex in Hong Kong that she won at the age of 33, beating out more than 538 other entries. Before Hadid could get the project going, however, the developer went bankrupt and the project was suspended, establishing a disappointing pattern wherein she would win a prestigious commission only to see her plans abandoned by developers and administrators. Hadid's frustration reached its peak with her explosive design for the Cardiff Bay Opera House in Wales, which caused such an uproar among conservatives that its construction was vetoed by the UK's Millennium Council after much political infighting.

Hadid's luck changed and she started to build, eventually winning the Pritzker Prize in 2004. The freestanding Rosenthal Center for Contemporary Art—the first American museum to be built by a solo female architect—opened in 2003, and was hailed for its innovative translucent skin and sculptural façade. Hadid is currently planning a large factory and offices for BMW in Leipzig, Germany, as well as a center for contemporary arts in Rome.

The Rosenthal Center for Contemporary Art, Cincinnati, Ohio.

Rather than presuming that flexibility depends on blandness, the building offers diverse conditions to choose from, each with a particular character. This creates a more engaging experience for the visitor. I believe architecture can be a catalyst for instigating and influencing the process of making, as well as viewing, art. I hope the space will instigate a new sense of possibility.

ZAHA HADID, ON THE ROSENTHAL CENTER FOR CONTEMPORARY ART

Zaha Hadid in London, 2004.

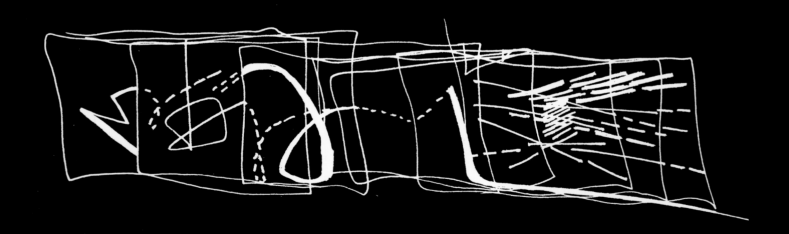

The Rosenthal Center for Contemporary Art, Cincinnati, Ohio.

JACQUES HERZOG
PIERRE DE MEURON

Jacques Herzog and Pierre de Meuron transcend the clichés of architecture by working with them. Although this impulse has led some critics to call them reactionary or conservative, the way they apply new techniques and treatments to modernist gestures has made their work fundamentally innovative and contemporary. Their goal is to recast the traditional in a way that makes it seem new and relevant once again.

The early work of this Basel-based studio was marked by the use of unique surface and light treatments on minimalist forms. The translucent exterior of a factory Herzog and de Meuron designed for the Swiss herbal cough-drop maker Ricola is silk-screened with leaves that filter daylight; a signal box next to the main railway station in Basel is covered with copper strips that resemble high-tech Venetian blinds; and the Eberswalde Library—structurally a simple rectangular box—is silk-screened with an image by German photographer Thomas Ruff. Meanwhile, the studio's luminous Prada Aoyama Epicenter in Tokyo, which opened in 2003, has become a local landmark.

Herzog and de Meuron's more recent work has moved away from the rigor of their early forms, although, the studio still embraces new materials and techniques in a way that earned them a Pritzker Prize in 2001. Of the six finalists in the competition to design a new museum for the Tate Gallery's collection of modern and contemporary art in a former power station, Herzog and de Meuron were the only ones to suggest leaving the building largely intact. By harnessing the power and energy of the building—a move likened by Herzog to the Japanese martial art aikido—the partners were able to create a space that makes use of the Victorian façade and main turbine room while still being wholly new.

**Jacques Herzog and Pierre de Meuron,
at an exhibition of their work in Montreal, 2003.**

Depending on where the viewer is standing, the body of the building looks more like a crystal or an archaic type of building with a saddle roof. The ambivalent, always changing, and oscillating character of the building's identity is heightened by the sculptural effect of its glazed surface structure. These differing geometries generate faceted reflections, which enable viewers to see constantly changing pictures and almost cinematographic perspectives of Prada products, the city, and themselves.

JACQUES HERZOG AND PIERRE DE MEURON, ON THE PRADA AOYAMA EPICENTER

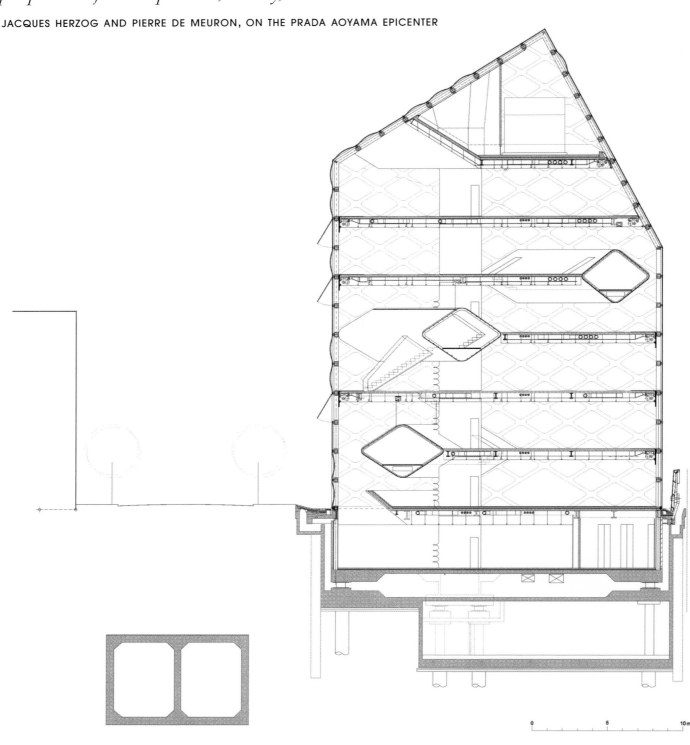

0   5   10m

Prada Aoyama Epicenter, Tokyo.

STEVEN HOLL

In an age that seems unable to appreciate an artist or work until it has been labeled, Steven Holl's architecture refuses to be tied down. Its idiosyncrasy, in fact, was originally a source of frustration for the New York–based architect. During the late '80s and early '90s, Holl won a series of major competitions only to see his designs put suspended once the practicalities of building took hold. But with the construction of the Museum of Contemporary Art in Helsinki and the Makuhari housing project in Chiba, Japan, Holl's luck changed: his theory-based architecture—developed at the University of Washington at Seattle and the Architectural Association in London, and subsequently promoted in his classroom at Columbia University since 1981—began to be part of the built world.

At its core, Holl's architecture is a true heir to modernism. His use of the golden section in his design for Kiasma, the Museum of Contemporary Art in Helsinki, distinctly references Le Corbusier, who also made use of Greek ideals in his work. Yet Holl is by no means a modernist. Instead of reducing space to its purest forms, Holl uses architecture to maximize space and the ways in which people perceive it.

In his plan for Simmons Hall at M.I.T., Holl disregarded the site's master plan, which called for a modernist block, and turned the concept inside out, basing his design instead on what he calls "porosity," an idea of openess that encompasses the majority of Holl's architecture. Although it is tempting to think of Steven Holl as the arche-typal artist, venturing deep within himself to uncover an arcane formal language, his work is not architecture for the sake of architecture, but is deeply involved with human experience.

The sponge concept for the new undergraduate residence hall transforms a porous building morphology via a series of programmatic and bio-technical functions.

STEVEN HOLL, ON SIMMONS HALL AT M.I.T.

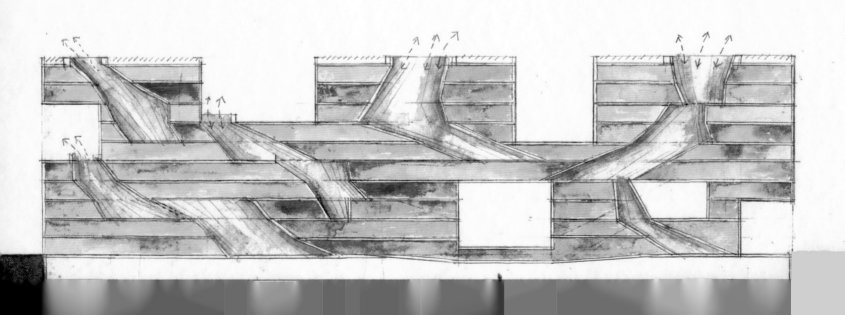

Simmons Hall, Massachusetts
Institute of Technology, Cambridge.
Following pages: Steven Holl
in his Manhattan studio, 2001.

FONDATION FRANÇOIS PINAU
ILE SEGUIN, PARIS

STEVEN HOL...

HANS HOLLEIN

Hans Hollein is used to upsetting people. When the Austrian architect first designed his celebrated Haas Haus building on Vienna's Stephansplatz, the subsequent cultural uproar resulted in the repeal of an ordinance requiring any building in the city's inner ring to match the style and form of surrounding historical structures. This conservation law had the effect of preventing the construction of modern buildings that challenged Viennese tradition, and whose result was an urban landscape that was more museum piece than dynamic environment.

Just two minutes from the Haas Haus, which was completed in 1990, is the building that launched Hollein's career in 1964—a twelve-foot-wide candle store and showroom that earned him the Reynolds Memorial Award (which was more money than the project's budget). Following the success of the Retti Candleshop, Hollein received commissions for other small, intimate spaces, and established a reputation for an eccentric kind of elegance that freely draws from modern and historical elements and mixes a classical vocabulary with an industrial sleekness.

Museum buildings created for the cities of Monchengladbach and Frankfurt express Hollein's characteristic wit and reverence for art—his first love. But civic discourse tends to be heated when his projects are unveiled. Frankfurt's Museum of Modern Art was a point of contention for certain citizens, who thought that the pink, wedge-shaped building looked more like a slice of birthday cake than a repository for cultural artifacts. Hollein's eclectic style can be traced to his education at Vienna's Academy of Fine Arts, the Illinois Institute of Technology, and the University of California at Berkeley. This combination of old- and new-world influences has led Hollein to create pioneering works that reflect a distinctly Viennese sensibility wherever he designs.

Hans Hollein in his studio in Vienna, 2003.
Following pages: The Haas Haus,
Vienna, Austria.

The Haas Haus signifies the dialectic between past and future. It stands for the continuous transformation of a living city, a city with a history of 2,000 years—2,000 years of activity and aspiration, of a population expressing themselves also in buildings.

HANS HOLLEIN, ON THE HAAS HAUS

ARATA ISOZAKI

Born in 1931, Arata Isozaki came of age in a Japan that had not only been decimated by World War II, but also had found that many of its ancient traditions and customs were suddenly illegal due to a new constitution. In this cultural vacuum, Isozaki came to the same conclusion that the American postmodernists would years later: that in a rootless time, modernism's struggle for universal precepts is at best naïve and at worst dangerous. In contrast to the American postmodernists, though, who turned to classical forms in order to regain a sense of stability, Isozaki's work uses an eclectic vocabulary that borrows equally from baroque and modernist styles in order to acknowledge that we are at the beginning of the future, instead of at the end of the past.

Richly varied, Isozaki's career began in the late 1950s when, after graduating from Japan's elite University of Tokyo, he joined the firm of Kenzo Tange, who was in the process of redefining Japanese architecture. After founding his own firm in 1963, Isozaki received the commission to design the Oita Medical Hall. Like many of his early works, the building profoundly shows the influence of Tange but also illustrates Isozaki's interest in investigating basic architectural forms—spheres, pyramids, and columns. Isozaki's large and controversial 1983 Tsukuba Center Building—which references Western antiquity from Egypt to Rome and essentially reproduces Michelangelo's Campidoglio in reverse—is intended as a reflection on emptiness that borrows Western conventions in order to criticize the resurgence of Japanese nationalism. His first major Western project, the 1986 Museum of Contemporary Art in Los Angeles, uses pyramids, cylinders, and cubes to create beautiful, pure spaces, and well demonstrates how Isozaki has confronted the dilemmas facing contemporary Japanese architecture.

The patterns of circulation of the two blocks standing in opposition to each other are like two spirals, giving the whole a flowing pattern of interaction. As a reference to the Golden Rule and concept of duality of East and West, it constitutes one of the fundamental concepts underlying this building.

ARATA ISOZAKI, ON THE LOS ANGELES MUSEUM OF CONTEMPORARY ART

Arata Isozaki in his studio in Minato-ku, Tokyo, 2003.

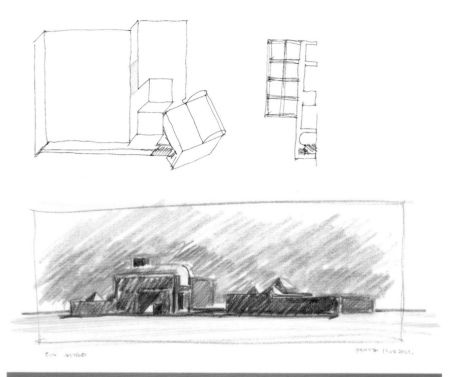

The Los Angeles Museum of Contemporary Art.

TOYO ITO

Ever since founding his first studio in Tokyo in 1971, Toyo Ito has been known for creating extreme concept buildings. Perhaps his best-known design is the Sendai Mediatheque in Japan. In this building, traditional structure has been pared away, leaving a glass container with a few internal walls that are supported by random groups of tubular columns. The building expresses Ito's fascination with lightness and his desire to strip away anything that reminds him of gravity.

For the 65-year-old Japanese architect, the human body exists on two levels: the physical body, which seeks the light and air found in nature, and a new virtual body that responds to the electronic environment by seeking information. The challenge for architecture and urban design is to integrate these two bodies. Linking the old and the new, the local with the exotic, is something that Ito did expertly in his pavilion for the Belgian city of Brugge, which was designated as Europe's cultural capital of 2002 by the European Commission. The city's residents loved the temporary structure so much that they opted to preserve it. Another of Ito's archetypal works is the Tower of Winds, a 1986 commission by the city of Yokohama, which appears to be made of solid aluminum during the daytime, but becomes illuminated from within at night and fluctuates according to wind and noise, giving the building an appearance of fluidity and movement.

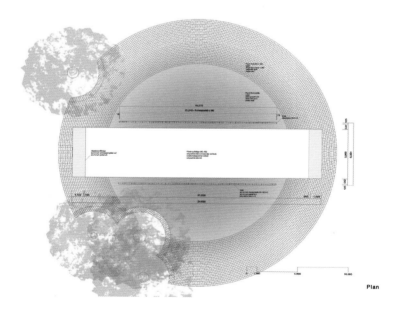

Plan

Just like other ancient capitals, Brugge is wavering between the responsibility of preserving historical views and the desire to flower in its potential as a contemporary city. What we have been asked is to show the possibility of contemporary architecture built in a historical content.

TOYO ITO, ON THE BRUGGE PAVILION

Toyo Ito in his studio in Shibuya-ku, Tokyo, 2003.
Following pages: The Brugge Pavilion, Brugge, Belgium.

PHILIP JOHNSON

When the Pritzker Prize was established in 1979 as the "Nobel Prize for Architecture," the choice of Philip Johnson as its first laureate seemed obvious. The ultimate connoisseur, Johnson began his career as the first director of the Museum of Modern Art in New York, where he became an active proponent of the work of Mies van der Rohe and Le Corbusier and was instrumental in bringing the International Style to an American audience. Not content with his role as a critic and curator, however, Johnson returned to Harvard to study architecture, and in 1949 built his iconic Glass House, in New Canaan. Inspired by Mies van der Rohe's 1947 Farnsworth House, the Glass House—whose original design was Johnson's master's thesis—took minimalism to its extreme.

Johnson went on to collaborate with Mies on the design of the Seagram Building, but toward the late 1950s he became frustrated with the formal constraints of architectural asceticism. Johnson declared that architects could not ignore history, and started looking to the past for sources of inspiration. Although Johnson did not point modernism in an alternative direction, he broke the rules in order to escape its rigidity.

Johnson spent much of the 1970s and '80s experimenting with different styles. Works such as the AT&T Building and Pennzoil Place succeeded in breaking up the previously rectilinear New York skyline, ensuring that no sense of order could ever be reimposed on it. Over the course of a long and varied career, Johnson has practiced architecture as collage—seeking the best in all available forms in order to both comment on and redefine the terms of architecture.

This place is about landscape. Over the years, when a client has requested a design like the Glass House, I have always asked first, "Do you have land?" People think the house is about glass, but the basic building block is trees.

PHILIP JOHNSON, ON THE GLASS HOUSE

Philip Johnson in the sculpture gallery on his property
in New Canaan, Connecticut, 1999.
Following pages: The Glass House, New Canaan, Connecticut.

REM KOOLHAAS

For Rem Koolhaas, a building's program is the starting point from which form is generated; any beauty that arrives during a project's conceptualization and design process is a byproduct rather than a goal. Research is critical to the Rotterdam-based Koolhaas, who has added a think tank—dedicated to investigating and developing new approaches to architecture and urbanism—to his already burgeoning studio, Office for Metropolitan Architecture (OMA). Koolhaas also practices this concept-based approach to architecture at his ongoing seminar at Harvard, the Project for the City, where he and his team of students investigate urban issues. The product of the seminar is a series of books that brings together images, maps, charts, and essays in order to create new ways of approaching global trends.

Despite his reputation for theory, Koolhaas is defiantly not a paper architect. He thrives on the interplay between the architect's ideas, the client's desires, and the site's restrictions, and he has built such landmarks as the 1992 Kunsthal Rotterdam, the 1994 master plan and Grand Palais for Lille, and the 1997 Educatorium at Utrecht University. His ability to create clarity out of constraint can be seen most clearly in a house he designed in Bordeaux for a newspaper publisher and his family. The husband, who had been paralyzed in an automobile accident, wanted a house that could accommodate his needs. Instead of designing around this requirement, Koolhaas built it into the very structure of the house via a circular platform that performs a dual function as both the publisher's study and as an elevator that connects him to both floors of the house.

On a larger scale, Koolhaas uses the limitations of cities as the starting point for a new sort of urbanism. His iconic book, *Delirious New York*, proposed an urban design for a time of chaos, one that seeks not to focus on previously defined urban centers, but to embrace its sprawl and inherent instability.

Rem Koolhaas and his firm,
Office for Metropolitan Architecture, Rotterdam, 2004.

Kunsthal Rotterdam, the Netherlands.

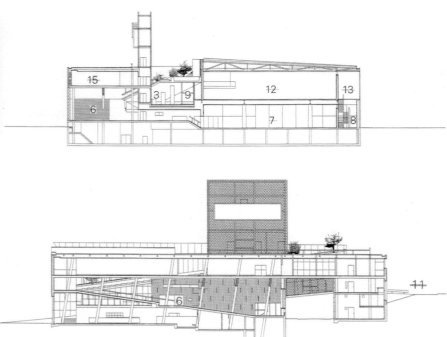

The building was conceived as a square crossed by two routes: one, a road running east/west, parallel to the Maasboulevard; the other, a public ramp extending the north/south axis of the Museum Park. With these givens, and the fact that these crossings would divide the square into four parts, the challenge became: how to design a museum as four autonomous projects—a sequence of contradictory experiences that would nevertheless form a continuous spiral. In other words, how to imagine a spiral in four separate squares.

REM KOOLHAAS, ON THE KUNSTHAL ROTTERDAM

RICARDO LEGORRETA

With its extensive fountain courtyards and brightly colored plaster walls and columns, the 1968 Hotel Camino Real in Mexico City established Ricardo Legorreta as one of the few architects capable of taking the abstract, vernacular manner of Luis Barragán from domestic to monumental scale. Whether beachfront hotels, factories, or museums, Legorreta's designs have been solid constructions with thick walls and few apertures, most often dressed in bright colors—especially red. They have been designed to fit into the natural environment and emphasize the supremacy of solids over voids and the use of color to offset walls. The resulting buildings promote a sense of privacy and enclosure.

Educated at the National University of Mexico, Legorreta established his practice in Mexico City in 1963. Although most of his buildings can be found in Mexico, in the past decade Legorreta has received numerous commissions for libraries and museums in the United States and Europe, including the Children's Discovery Museum in San José, California; the San Antonio Main Library; the University of Chicago Residence Halls; and the Fashion and Textile Museum in London. He was recently able to develop his ideas on communal housing into the design and construction of social housing units in Madrid's La Latina district, and the Zocalo development in Santa Fe, New Mexico. In 1994, Legorreta completed the construction of the Metropolitan Cathedral in Managua, designed to accommodate festivals of up to 100,000 people.

The search for an individual personality for the hotel was motivated by my reaction against the coldness and lack of friendliness of ordinary hotels. All the spaces were designed to provide a sense of luxury, not because of the materials used, but because of their spaciousness. The atmosphere of dignity that is created is based on the use of water, light, and color, which are characteristic of Mexican architecture.

RICARDO LEGORRETA, ON THE HOTEL CAMINO REAL

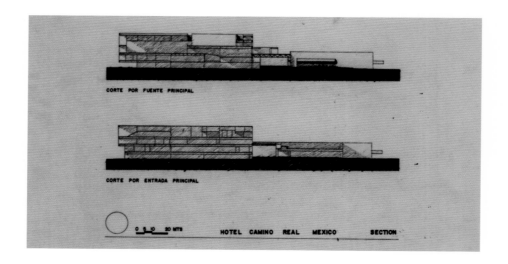

Ricardo Legorreta in his studio in Mexico City, 2003.

The Hotel Camino Real, Mexico City.

DANIEL LIBESKIND

Perhaps the only architect who can boast of having performed at Carnegie Hall, Daniel Libeskind originally intended to be a musician. Born in Lodz, Poland, in 1946, Libeskind studied piano from an early age—an activity that intensified when his family emigrated to Israel when he was 11, and again when they came to the United States two years later. Despite forging a notable reputation as a young concert pianist, Libeskind jettisoned his musical career in favor of architecture. In 1970, he received his architectural degree from Cooper Union and, two years later, a postgraduate degree in the History and Theory of Architecture at the School of Comparative Studies at Essex University in England.

Before winning the commission to design the much-anticipated Jewish Museum in Berlin in 1989, Libeskind was one of the world's best-known non-building architects. The Jewish Museum's zigzag-shaped building—in part, an architectural response to Arnold Schönberg's unfinished opera *Moses and Aaron*—opened to great acclaim after ten years of construction and political wrangling. Libeskind went on to receive other important cultural commissions, including the 1998 Felix Nussbaum Museum in Osnabrück, Germany, and the 2002 Imperial War Museum North in Manchester, England. Libeskind's winning design for the master plan of the World Trade Center site—which includes the Freedom Tower that will be the world's tallest building at 1,776 feet—has elevated the architect to the world stage, where he seems more than comfortable performing.

The Imperial War Museum North deals with the conflicts that have shaped the twentieth century and those that will continue to shape the future. The building brings together culture and regeneration, craft and design, in order to give the public a striking emblem that in an instant illuminates both tradition and the new.

DANIEL LIBESKIND, ON THE IMPERIAL WAR MUSEUM NORTH

Daniel Libeskind in his Manhattan studio, 2003.

The Imperial War Museum North, Manchester, England.

GREG LYNN

For better or worse, Greg Lynn has become associated with "blobs." Using computer technology adapted from digital animation and automotive-design programs, Lynn creates complex shapes that emphasize curves and continuity rather than straight lines and borders. After earning his master's in architecture from Princeton University in 1988, Lynn spent four years working in the office of Peter Eisenman before establishing his own practice, Greg Lynn FORM, in Hoboken, New Jersey. Moving four years later to Venice, California, in order to take advantage of the proximity to aeronautic, automobile, and film industry technologies, Lynn has become known for combining his love of philosophy and theory with the realities of design and construction through teaching and writing, as well as running a thriving architecture practice.

In his 1999 design for the Korean Presbyterian Church of New York, in Sunnyside, Queens, Lynn—in conjunction with Garofalo Architects and Michael McInturf Architects—transformed the WPA-era Knickerbocker Laundry Factory into a church and community center that features a stunning undulating roofline, serpentine stairways, and an armadillo-like exterior. All of these elements were designed digitally. Collaborating remotely with other architects around the country, Lynn's studio has partnered with McInturf and GBBN Architects on a new building for the Cincinnati Country Day School; with Peter Eisenman on a "Vision Plan" for Rutgers University; and with United Architects on a plan for the new World Trade Center.

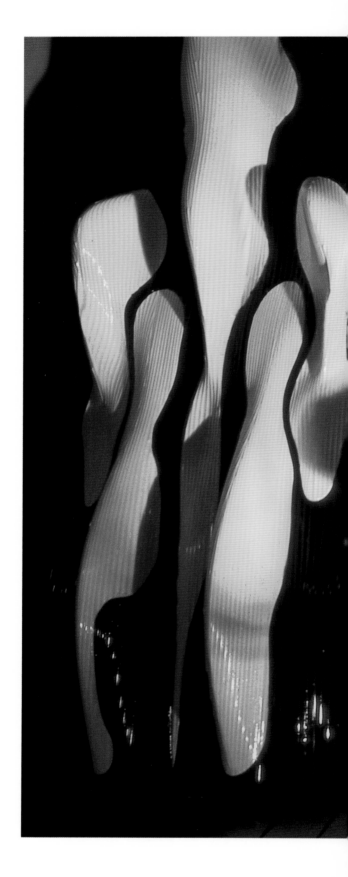

Greg Lynn in his Los Angeles studio, 2004.
Following pages: The Korean Presbyterian Church of New York, Sunnyside, Queens.

Not only did our clients ask us to convert a laundry factory into a church, but they asked that it not be a Catholic cathedral or a Scandinavian modern church, but a Korean Presbyterian Church. Producing a sacred space with all of the atmosphere and meaning of a classical church but with a completely new vocabulary of interior and exterior shapes and materials was a great opportunity for a first commission.

GREG LYNN, ON THE KOREAN PRESBYTERIAN CHURCH OF NEW YORK

RODOLFO MACHADO
JORGE SILVETTI

In a city like Boston, with its rich cultural and architectural history, there is a temptation to preserve the landscape to the extent of embalming it. Oddly enough, though, Rodolfo Machado and Jorge Silvetti have established one of the country's most progressive architecture studios smack in the center of Boston

Although both Machado and Silvetti grew up in traditional Argentina, they received their Masters degrees from Berkeley in the early 1970s—a time of social and cultural upheaval that profoundly informed the architects' thinking. In addition to their architectural practice, the pair has devoted themselves to teaching, with Machado chairing the architecture department at the Rhode Island School of Design before becoming a member of the faculty at Harvard University's Graduate School of Design, where Silvetti has taught since 1975.

Up until fairly recently, Machado and Silvetti were known as inventive stylists who, due to the quirks of fate, never quite managed to get any of their designs built. When their luck changed and the pair began receiving major commissions, they revealed themselves to be adept at creating modernist contextual architecture—a design approach that incorporates buildings into their surroundings without the rampant quotations that define postmodernism at its worst. Works such as the 2001 Honan-Allston Branch of the Boston Public Library and the partners' 2003 One Western Avenue, a dormitory for Harvard University in Allston, have exhibited their capacity for creating bold geometric shapes while still preserving the integrity of the surrounding area.

One Western Avenue,
Harvard University, Allston, Massachusetts.

The building's configuration and image are based on our interpretations of its physical context along the river: the early-twentieth-century, five-story, brick-clad, U-shaped neo-Georgian courtyard houses and the mid-twentieth-century, twenty-story, concrete-paneled modern towers.

JORGE MACHADO AND RODOLFO SILVETTI, ON ONE WESTERN AVENUE

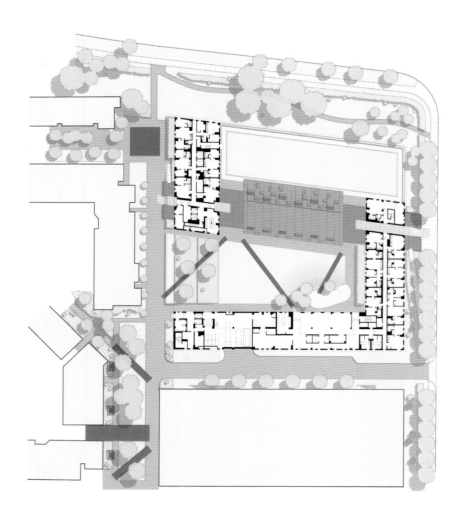

Jorge Silvetti and Rodolfo Machado
in Battery Park, New York, 2001.

The project reverses the message sent by a society that routinely communicates its disregard for the young by educating them in carelessly arranged, temporary bungalows surrounded by impenetrable chain link fencing. At Diamond Ranch, the high school's goals of educational flexibility and social interaction between students, teachers, and administration are expressed in a thoughtful and heterogeneous design.

THOM MAYNE, ON THE DIAMOND RANCH HIGH SCHOOL

THOM MAYNE

Thom Mayne
in his Los Angeles studio, 2004.

In the world of architecture, 53 is fairly young. This was the age at which Thom Mayne—considered by many to be the bad boy of L.A. architecture—came into his own with a winning design for Diamond Ranch High School in Pomona, California. Although Mayne had built a few major works before—notably L.A.'s Cedars-Sinai Comprehensive Cancer Center Hospital—this 1999 campus marked his grand entry into the world of built architecture, and even garnered comparisons to Thomas Jefferson's University of Virginia campus.

As one of the founders of the cutting-edge Southern California Institute of Architecture—and one of three principals of the Santa Monica–based studio Morphosis, which thrived on theories of flux and dynamism—Mayne acquired a reputation in the 1980s for producing brilliant and highly esoteric paper architecture that won him a number of awards and small commissions for architectural connoisseurs. Characterized by his use of such industrial materials as metal, concrete, and glass, Mayne became known for creating forms that aggressively jut out into public spaces. As a major built work, the Diamond Ranch High School confirmed Mayne's potential. Characterized by a rhythmic movement between fluidity and angularity, the Diamond Ranch High School integrates into the site's topography.

With the success of the Diamond Ranch School, Mayne has hit his stride and has a number of major commissions in the works: plans for an Olympic Village along the East River in Long Island City (in the event New York is chosen for the 2012 games); a federal office building in San Francisco whose metal cladding and lack of windows will enable natural ventilation; and a new building for the Cooper Union in New York's East Village.

Diamond Ranch High School,
Pomona, California.

RICHARD MEIER

Ask Richard Meier where he picked up his renowned modernist sensibility, and the answer may have more to do with art than with architecture. Before becoming an architect, Richard Meier was a painter, even sharing a studio with Frank Stella. So, it is not surprising that his most respected designs have been for buildings that contain art—whether public spaces like Atlanta's High Museum, the Barcelona Museum of Contemporary Art, and the Gagosian Gallery in Beverly Hills, or residences that house world-class private art collections.

Meier's first architectural commission after graduating from Cornell University in 1963 was for his parent's house in New Jersey. But it was actually another residence—the Smith House in Darien, Connecticut—that thrust Meier into national prominence in 1967, and established his hallmark style of cube-like structures, clean lines, and white surfaces. Yet although Meier made his first impressions designing residences, it has been his public commissions, including the New Harmony Atheneum and the Jubilee Church in Rome, that have made the biggest impact on the contemporary landscape.

Upon being awarded the Pritzker Prize in 1984 at the unprecedented age of 49, Meier was widely hailed for the clarity of vision and execution that he brought to every project. That same year he was awarded the "commission of the century," the $1 billion Getty Center in Los Angeles. A shining white complex of buildings situated on its own scenic perch in the Santa Monica Mountains, the Getty opened to critical and public acclaim in 1997.

In the case of his striking residential towers in New York's West Village, which were completed in 2002, Meier has carved out a calm space on the edge of Manhattan to meditate on the extended artwork that is his city.

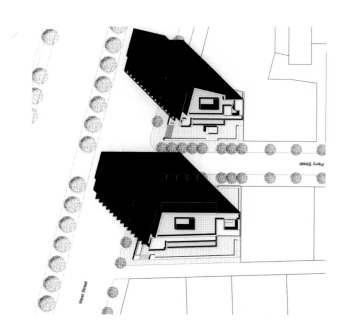

These twin residential towers, filled with light and air, on the north and south corners of Perry and West streets in Greenwich Village, are the new buildings I have designed in Manhattan. The façades are composed of insulating laminated glass and white metal panels with shadow boxes that express the individual floor plates. The apartments, one per floor, afford unobstructed panoramic views of the city, the Hudson River, and the New Jersey riverfront. Their transparent minimal form is a striking addition to the New York City skyline.

RICHARD MEIER, ON 173/176 PERRY STREET

Richard Meier at his house
in East Hampton, New York, 2003.

ERIC OWEN MOSS

Born and raised in Los Angeles, Eric Owen Moss practices architecture in a style that is fundamentally linked to his hometown. In the same way that James Joyce cannibalized the language and culture of his native Dublin in order to find new and unique ways of personal expression, Moss has invigorated L.A.'s urban landscape by reinterpreting its vernacular forms. Since establishing his studio in 1973, Moss' biggest achievement has been his wholesale urban renewal project in L.A.'s Culver City, which boasts three sites and forty-three buildings in various stages of construction—a real-life architectural laboratory for his highly complex, aggressive geometric forms.

In a city characterized by sprawl, it is only through sheer force of will that an architect can make his presence known. In Petal House, one of his first projects to gather international attention, Moss transformed a conventional two-story 1940s bungalow by opening up its roof in a way that resembled a sunflower. Rearticulating the banal by using common materials such as particle board, steel bars, and clay sewer pipes to stand in for more expensive and respected materials, Moss' architecture doesn't harken back to modernism's fantasies of utopia. Instead, it acknowledges that any urban renewal project must incorporate the fragmentation and uncertainty inherent to contemporary city life. In addition to transforming the landscape of his sprawling hometown, Moss also has made a considerable impact on its intellectual life as director of the Southern California Institute of Architecture since 2002.

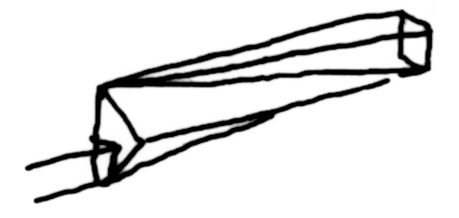

Eric Owen Moss in Los Angeles, 2002.

132

The aspiration was to investigate a changing exterior form and a varying interior space, to construct a building that remakes both outside and inside.

ERIC OWEN MOSS, ON THE STEALTH BUILDING

The Stealth Building, Culver City, California.

ENRIQUE NORTEN

Enrique Norten has dotted his native Mexico City with large, luminous, minimalist works that use glass and metal in a visually transcendent way. When not in his newly opened New York studio, Norten lives in Mexico City's Condesa neighborhood, where he grew up. It was in this same neighborhood that he established TEN Arquitectos in 1985 and began evolving a design practice that aimed to synthesize local and global aspects of contemporary life in seamless forms. Over the past nineteen years, Norten has designed a range of hometown projects, including the conversion of the 2002 Hotel Habita that used a translucent glass façade to envelope the existing building; and the 1998 downtown multiuse corporate offices and canteen for the broadcasting giant Televisa, which features a curvy metal sheath that elegantly comprises both walls and roof.

More recently, Norten's design for the JVC Convention Center on the outskirts of Guadalajara consists of an enormous free-span glass dome. These bold stabs at redefining Mexican architecture have recently brought the Cornell graduate his first important U.S commissions, including Harlem Park—the first skyscraper to be built in Harlem—and the Brooklyn Visual and Performing Arts Library in the BAM Cultural District.

The old structure achieves a new identity because of its new wrapper—a frosted glass envelope composed of rectangular glass panels, which exist beyond the original façade. From a distance, the new façade appears to be an expressionless mask, but this impression is undermined at closer range, as a play of shadows appears—the shadowed walkways, balconies and guests become visible.

ENRIQUE NORTEN, ON THE HOTEL HABITA

Enrique Norten at his home in Mexico City, 2003.

The Hotel Habita,
Mexico City.

JEAN NOUVEL

In the late 1980s, Jean Nouvel proposed the Tour Sans Fin (the Endless Tower) for La Défense, a business district at the western edge of Paris. Slated to be a 350-meter-high sleek cylinder that would rise from a solid base and become increasingly transparent toward the top—in effect disappearing into the sky—this unrealized project was emblematic of Nouvel's ambition, which he has said is to "make things nonexistent."

Nouvel has practiced architecture in Paris since he received his diploma from the École des Beaux-Arts in 1972, founding his first studio in 1984 and his current studio ten years later. Based in the Bastille district of Paris, Nouvel's firm is presently involved in more than forty projects, including museums for Paris, Rio, Quatar, and Seoul; symphony halls for Lucerne and Copenhagen; and a theater for Minneapolis.

The best known and loved of Nouvel's completed buildings is his 1987 Arab World Institute in Paris, which features a wall of intricate metal irises in the guise of traditional Islamic patterns that open and close to control the level and intensity of light entering the building. His design for the Fondation Cartier, also in Paris, is an example of the architect's perennial quest to merge inside and outside. The Fondation Cartier has an extra glass plane that both acts as a façade and works to preserve a 200-year-old cedar of Lebanon planted by Chateaubriand in 1823.

Given that the Arab World Institute is the showcase for the Arab world in Paris, I wanted it to remain a Western building, while also integrating symbolic cultural elements. The architectural elements incorporated are therefore at the forefront of these two cultures: squares, polygons, a geometry that recalls the Alhambra (in Grenada) and the omnipresence of water.

JEAN NOUVEL, ON THE ARAB WORLD INSTITUTE

Jean Nouvel at the Mercer Hotel in New York, 2002.

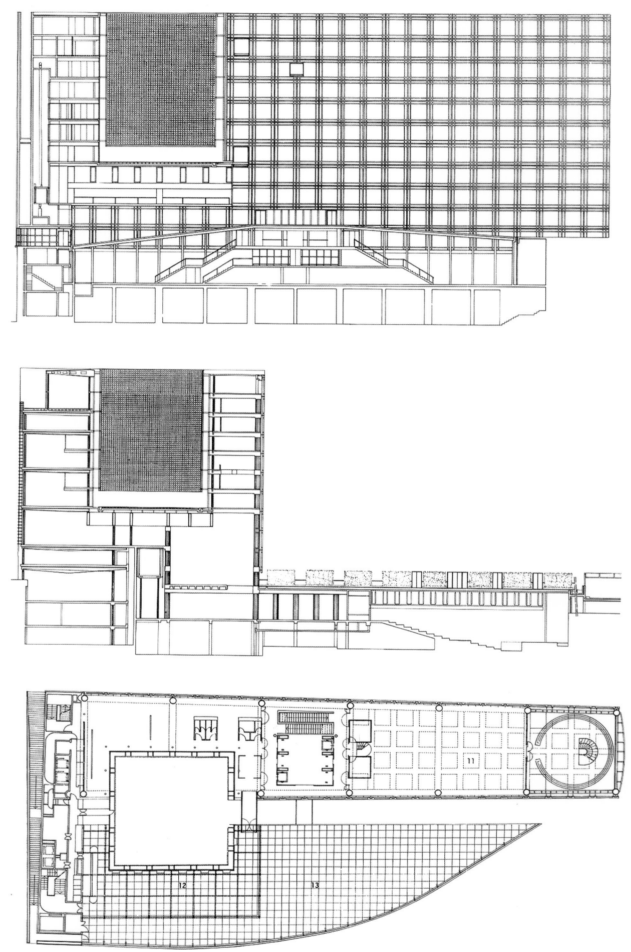

The Arab World Institute, Paris.

WILLIAM PEDERSEN

Since its founding in 1976, Kohn Pedersen Fox Associates has emerged as a serious challenger to the venerable Skidmore, Owings & Merrill for dominance in the realm of corporate architecture. As principal design partner, William Pedersen has distinguished the firm by merging architectural originality with a profound respect for the context in which a building exists. Rather than establish a distinctive style, Pedersen has let the demands of the client and the site dictate the form of his buildings.

Pedersen received his bachelor of architecture from the University of Minnesota in 1961, and went on to the Massachusetts Institute of Technology, where he earned his master's in 1963. Since then, he has established a practice based on assemblage and collage, with the result that his buildings make use of the past without being wholly enthralled with it. Early works, such as 333 Wacker Drive in Chicago, feature a visual language that is at once classical and abstract in the manner of a Brancusi structure.

More mature works, such as Rockefeller Center West, accommodate the iconic 1930s skyscrapers of the original Rockefeller Center, as well as the complex's newer office buildings from the 1960s. Pedersen has received numerous National Honor Awards from the AIA for such projects as his 2003 Baruch College building in New York, the 1998 World Bank headquarters in Washington, D.C., and the 1997 Procter & Gamble campus in Cincinnati.

Served by six oversized elevators, which stop every third floor, the various departments of the college are disposed about an internal space that twists as it rises throughout the height of the building to a great window high on the building's south side. Flooded with natural light, this space is a vertical interpretation of the traditional college quadrangle.

WILLIAM PEDERSEN, ON BARUCH COLLEGE

William Pedersen at Baruch College in New York, 2002.

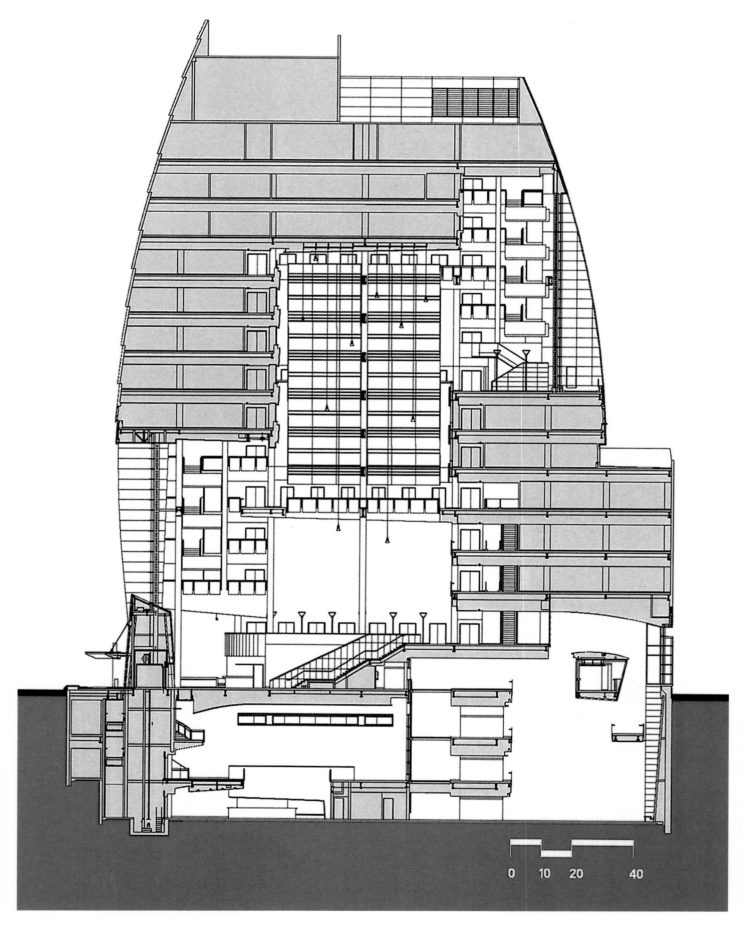

Baruch College, New York.

I.M. Pei in his office in Midtown Manhattan, 1998.

I.M. PEI

Through a series of sleek, elegant structures, I.M. Pei has established himself as one of the world's most recognizable architects, known for adroitly balancing the pleasures of art with the demands of commerce. Born in Canton, China, in 1917, Ieoh Ming Pei was sent to the United States in 1935 to study. After receiving a bachelor in architecture at the Massachusetts Institute of Technology, Pei went on to earn a master's at Harvard, where he studied under Walter Gropius. The strict modernism of the Bauhaus founder, however, was too restrictive for Pei, who looked to the freer forms of Le Corbusier and Marcel Breuer for inspiration.

For seven years after graduating from Harvard, Pei worked for the developer William Zeckendorf, who taught him valuable lessons in urbanism, if not aesthetics. But it was only after Pei established his firm in 1955 that he came into his own artistically. An early work for the National Center for Atmospheric Research on a remote mesa in the Rocky Mountains gave the first inkling of Pei's prodigious talent. When Jacqueline Kennedy selected Pei in 1964 to design the John F. Kennedy Memorial Library, the young architect gained national recognition. Pei's design for the East Building of the National Gallery of Art in Washington, D.C., further proved that he could design monumental buildings that are highly accessible, while his 1993 limestone Four Seasons Hotel on 57th Street in Manhattan shows that he also has a keen sense for luxury.

Pei's breakthrough design for the Louvre, however, best showed that he could work in an idiom that was deeply respectful of history while still remaining a part of the late twentieth century. At a time when trendy architects were enthralled with postmodernism, Pei's adherence to the tenets of modernism caused critics to charge him with being out of date. But in recent years, Pei's ability to mine history while resisting the siren song of pastiche seems prescient.

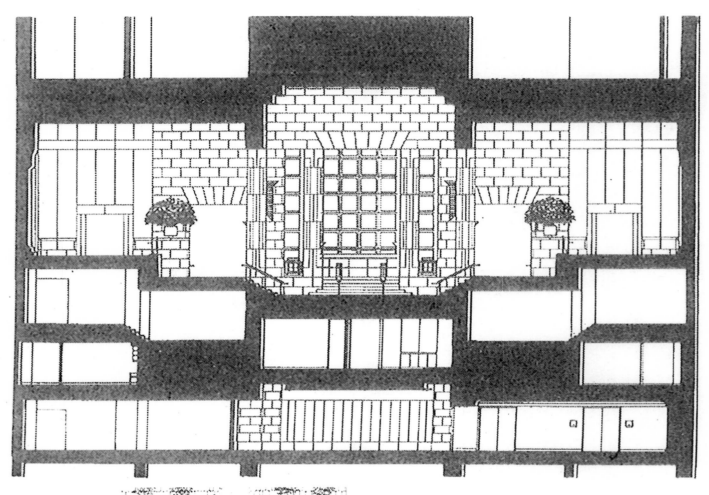

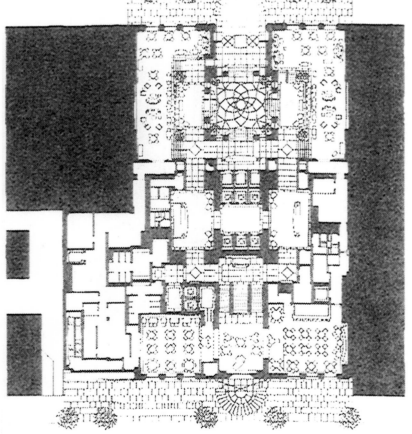

Located in one of the most fashionable areas in Midtown Manhattan, the Four Seasons was designed to continue the grand tradition of a former time when going to a hotel was an occasion. Its emphasis is not on workaday efficiency—checking in and out quickly—but on celebrating the luxury-hotel experience.

I.M. PEI, ON THE FOUR SEASONS HOTEL

The Four Seasons Hotel, New York.

CESAR PELLI

The Tower at 731 Lexington Avenue is an elegant crystalline form against the sky. At its base, Beacon Court, a public space, is an oasis in the city and marks an important place in Midtown Manhattan.

CESAR PELLI, ON 731 LEXINGTON AVENUE

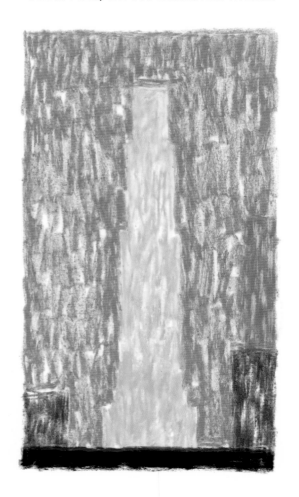

Argentine architect Cesar Pelli believes that there is more to the surface of things than meets the eye. As buildings become evermore dictated by zoning regulations and the needs of developers, Pelli chooses to focus his talents on the area where he can have the most creative impact: the color, texture, and reflectivity of a building's skin. His early projects were covered in colored reflective glass, creating prismatic patterns and reflections. These works, which include the polychromatic glass façade he designed for the Museum of Modern Art's apartment tower, were a precursor to designs that explore pattern through the use of more substantial materials such as brick and stone.

Since graduating from the University of Tucuman's school of architecture in his native Argentina and founding his studio in 1977 in New Haven, Connecticut (where he was dean of the Yale School of Architecture), Pelli has concerned himself with finding a form for the skyscraper that suits the spirit of our time. He seeks to create buildings that are more sumptuous than the spare Mies van der Rohe copies that sprung up in the 1960s and '70s, yet reject the easy thrills of postmodernism. His Petronas Towers in Malaysia and London's Canary Wharf tower have the grandeur of skyscrapers from the 1920s and '30s without reproducing or coyly quoting them.

Works such as the 1987 Winter Garden at the World Financial Center, with its iconic glass dome—as well as the elliptical courtyard at the 2004 731 Lexington Avenue—are soaring public spaces that could be the contemporary equivalent of Italian piazzas.

Cesar Pelli in his studio in New Haven, Connecticut, 2002.
Following pages: 731 Lexington Avenue, New York.

152

RENZO PIANO

Renzo Piano knows how to deal with crowds. He also knows how to create astonishingly elegant buildings that manifest an almost spiritual lightness of being. Since graduating from the School of Architecture at Milan Polytechnic in 1964 and establishing meaningful relationships with such design masters as Franco Albini and Jean Prouvé, Piano has amply demonstrated both of these often contradictory gifts. First there was his 1974 Pompidou Center, designed in collaboration with Richard Rogers, who was his studio partner until 1977, when Piano opened up a practice with the engineer Peter Rice. Rice's death in 1993, however, led Piano to start up his own architecture firm with offices in Paris and Genoa. Notable works include the $2 billion Kansai International Airport Terminal near Osaka; the master plan for the Potsdamer Platz in Berlin, which includes eight buildings; and the San Giovanni Rotondo church in Puglia, home of Italy's favorite modern saint, Padre Pio. A converging point for more than 7 million pilgrims a year, the church is a structure made out of local limestone that has been shaped into twenty-seven arches—a unique instance of high-tech handicraft.

Having grown up in Genoa in a family of builders, Piano's spent his childhood feeding a fascination with structures of nature and early culture: the young Piano collected photographs of spider webs and pre-industrial human shelters made from natural fibers. This preoccupation no doubt influenced his design for the Jean-Marie Tjibaou Cultural Center in Nouméa, New Caledonia, which consists of ten structures adapted from traditional Caledonian huts. While Piano's talent for designing structures with a high density of traffic is well documented, he has also crafted designs that meld with their background, including the Menil Collection in Houston—a 100,000-square-foot structure that looks like a two-story house from the outside—and the future Klee Museum in Bern, which will mimic the exact shape of the rolling alpine hills behind. Other recent projects include the 2001 Maison Hermès in Tokyo and the 2001 Niccolò Paganini auditorium in Parma, as well as a proposed 1,000-foot tall pyramidal London Bridge Tower and an addition to New York's Morgan Library.

When French Group Hermès chose the Ginza district, in the heart of Tokyo, for its Japanese headquarters, the project was both an aesthetic and technical challenge. How, in the architectural diversity of Tokyo, could a "landmark" building be conceived that would comply with the strict anti-seismic standards in Japan? The idea of a "magic lantern" lighting up in Ginza, like the ones traditionally hung at the doors of Japanese houses, soon made its way.

RENZO PIANO, ON THE MAISON HERMÈS

Renzo Piano in New York's Morgan Library, 2002.

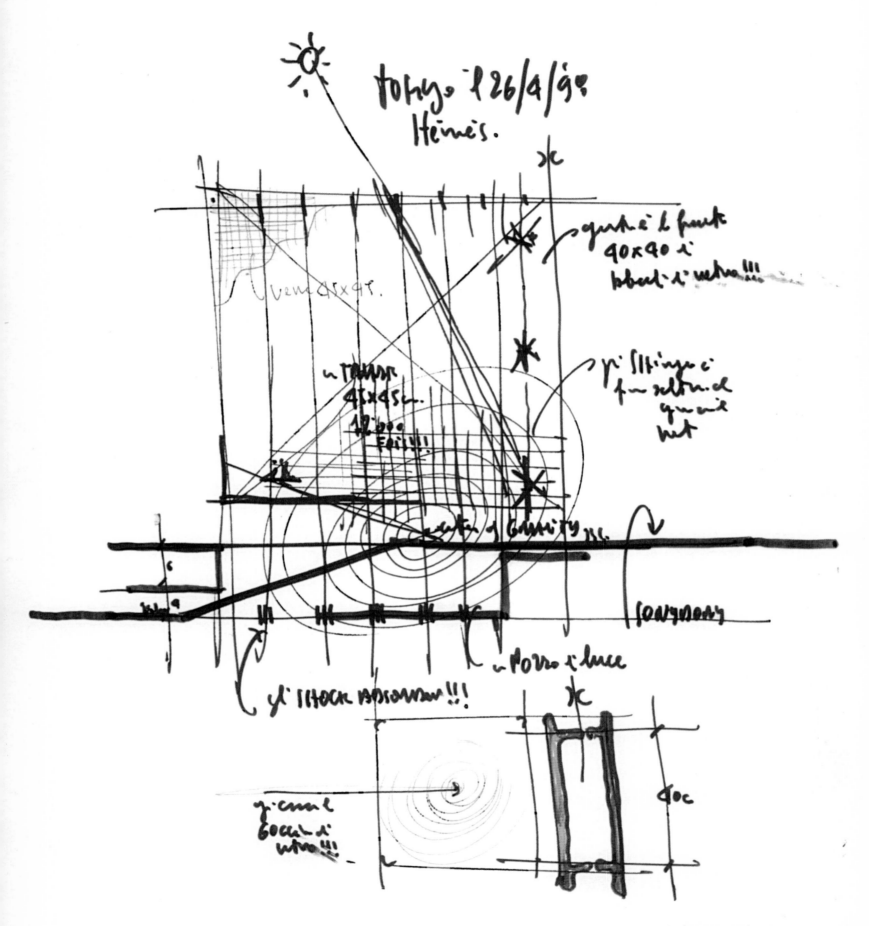

Maison Hermès, Tokyo.

CHRISTIAN DE PORTZAMPARC

Architecture is a profession that is notorious for rewarding an architect's contributions late in life. When the 50-year-old French architect Christian de Portzamparc was selected as the first member of the postwar generation to receive the Pritzker Prize in 1994, many in the architectural world were baffled. But the choice of Portzamparc was anything but arbitrary. With more than twenty built works to his name, this relatively young architect has already made a career out of bridging the gap between the extremes of modernist and postmodernist ideology.

Portzamparc first became interested in architecture at the age of 13, when he encountered the work of Le Corbusier. In 1962, he started studying architecture at the École des Beaux-Arts in Paris, but he soon doubted his chosen career. At the same time that other members of his peer group began questioning the impact of the modern movement on the city, Portzamparc began to feel that architecture had become too constrained by bureaucracy to effect social change. During this period of self-examination, he traveled to Greenwich Village, where he spent nine months in 1966 waiting tables and exploring New York's rich cultural landscape.

After returning to Paris to receive his degree, Portzamparc joined up with a group of sociologists studying how people interact with their neighborhoods. This experience fortified his conception of architecture as a social responsibility. Throughout his career, he has evolved this sentiment into a design philosophy that stresses a nuanced urban contextualism, which can be seen in buildings as varied as his 1995 City of Music in Paris's Parc de la Villette—a two-part complex dedicated in form and function to celebrating the musical arts—and his 1999 LVMH Tower in Manhattan, a cubist structure that unfolds in a pristine, prismatic manner.

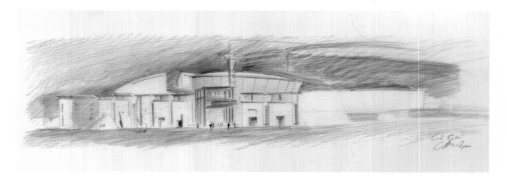

There is an aspect of the City of Music that seems important to me: the movement, the dissymmetry, and the re-conquest of the expressiveness of curves, obliques, and color that has appealed to me since the 1960s.

CHRISTIAN DE PORTZAMPARC, ON THE CITY OF MUSIC

Christian de Portzamparc, looking down at New York's 57th Street from within the LVMH Tower, 2003.

The City of Music, Paris.

ANTOINE PREDOCK

In 1954, an 18-year-old Antoine Predock arrived in Albuquerque for his freshman year at the University of New Mexico from his hometown of Lebanon, Missouri. It was his first exposure to the desert landscape that would become a major inspiration once he established his own architecture studio in Albuquerque. Much like the desert, Predock's architecture is stark yet responsive, simultaneously straightforward and elusive. The defining element of Predock's practice is its relationship to the spirit of the place in which it is built. Predock has a way of connecting his dramatic geometric forms with both the natural and cultural conditions of a place.

Predock's sensitivity to his own surroundings has given him an uncanny ability to interpret any site's context. Buildings like the angular Austin City Hall, situated on the shore of the Texas capital's Town Lake, and the wing-like Tang Teaching Museum and Art Gallery at Skidmore College in upstate New York have proven that Predock's genius isn't only his ability to channel the particular region's architectural traditions. Whether situated cheek to jowl with other beach houses like his 1991 residence in Venice or rising like a mountain out of the Wyoming landscape, as in his 1993 museum at the University of Wyoming, Predock's buildings are particularly attuned to where they are in time and space.

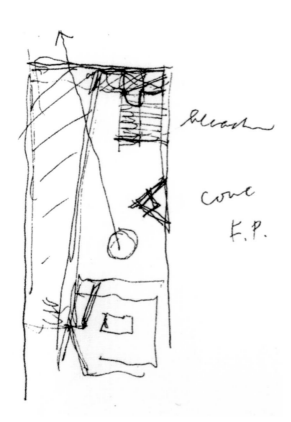

The Venice Beach House establishes a threshold between the Los Angeles Basin and the sea; between scenographic Los Angeles and transcendent geologic time. It is an observatory that tracks the setting sun as it becomes sunrise in Asia.

ANTOINE PREDOCK, ON THE VENICE BEACH HOUSE

Antoine Predock at his studio in Albuquerque, 2003.

The Venice Beach House,
Venice, California.

Wolf Prix in New York City, 2002.

WOLF PRIX

The rooftop extension to the law offices of Schuppich, Sporn, Winischhofer in Vienna perches over the top of a nineteenth-century building like a high-tech grasshopper. Until the late 1990s, this was the only major built work by Coop Himmelb(l)au, the experimental architecture and urban design studio started by the Viennese-born Wolf Prix and his Polish colleague Helmut Swiczinsky. Founded on the desire to create new structures that were free of formalism, the studio's name is a German play on words that translates into "Blue Sky Cooperative." Since its inception in 1968, Coop Himmelb(l)au has specialized in exploring the boundaries between public and private spaces, especially in its native city. The studio's SEG Apartment Tower, for instance, was based on the idea of stacking two houses on top of each other in a way that created a common "skylobby" at the intersection. Two years later, with its SEG Apartment Block, the studio reconfigured the traditional Viennese building complex by creating "air pockets" of space that served as common areas, private terraces, and gardens. In 2001, Coop Himmelb(l)au helped transform Gasometer B, one of four immense structures built in the nineteenth century to conceal Vienna's gas supply tanks. By placing a metal and glass shield outside of the existing circular landmark, the studio managed to aestheticize the space that exists between the structure's exterior and interior, as well as provide an event hall, offices, and apartments for everyday use.

The Gasometer is a very important project for Vienna because it established a new city center outside the main center, creating a tension between the old and the new, which is a very important part of modernism.

WOLF PRIX, ON GASOMETER B

The Gasometer B, Vienna, Austria.

LORD ROGERS

"Open" might be the term that best describes the architectural philosophy of Richard Rogers. This is most clearly evident in his 1977 design for the Centre Pompidou in Paris—which he created in collaboration with Renzo Piano—and the 1986 Lloyd's Building in London. The rationale behind the physical structure of both buildings is to allow the greatest amount of floor space for art or work in the center by putting the service elements boldly on the exterior—a feature that has earned his work the label of "engineering aesthetics." In their design for the Pompidou, Rogers and Piano insisted that more than half of the available site be used for a public piazza, with a shared Mediterranean belief that gatherings of people are what make cities interesting (Rogers was born in Florence into an Anglo-Italian family). The1986 Lloyd's Building structure of glass partitions with a central atrium gives the impression that the building is bustling with life.

Despite an unhappy childhood spent in British boarding schools—where teachers mistook his dyslexia for laziness and recommended that he become a policeman—Rogers has become one of Britain's most influential architects. After studying architecture at Yale and founding a studio with Norman Foster, he established the Richard Rogers Partnership in 1977 in London and created such renowned buildings as the Tribunal de Grande Instance in Bordeaux and the Millennium Dome in London. In the 1990s, Rogers turned his hand to city planning, producing master plans for the South Bank Centre in London, the Lu Jia Zui business district in Shanghai, the Terminal 5 at Heathrow Airport, and the former dockyards in Almada, Portugal. He was the recipient of a Knighthood for services to architecture in 1991 and a peerage in 1996.

Richard Rogers in his home in London, 2003.

Turning the plan inside out by placing service cores outside the main envelope offers two principal benefits: freeing the building of all internal obstructions, and making lifts and servicing systems more accessible for maintenance and future upgrades without disturbing the building's occupants.

RICHARD ROGERS, ON THE LLOYD'S OF LONDON BUILDING

Lloyd's of London.

LINDY ROY

As a child, Lindy Roy roamed the wilds of her native South Africa, imagining structures that would blend into the vast landscape. The experience turned out to be quite informative. The Columbia-educated architect is part of a generation of architects who combine futuristic computer-generated designs with new materials to energize the built landscape, whether on the African veldt or in downtown Tribeca.

Her projects include an "extreme" ski hotel in Alaska's Chugach Range, which can be reached only by skiing down a slope after being dropped onto a glacier from a helicopter, and a hotel spa set amidst hundreds of abandoned termite mounds in the Okavanga delta of Botswana.

Roy's designs often make use of high-tech finishes and organic curves, both of which create ingenious solutions to reutilizing space. In her Pool House in Sagaponac, Long Island, and in her Cycling Circuit Barn in upstate New York, she uses the playful characteristics of a pool and a bicycle path to unite the structures' exteriors and interiors. And in 2001, Roy was selected to transform P.S. 1/MoMA's outdoor playground in Queens from a concrete courtyard into a misty oasis. Roy's imagination also finds form in quintessentially urban interior spaces, such as the 2002 "reclamation" of a refrigerated meat-storage space for a bar, and a 12,000-square-foot showroom for Vitra which features flexible curtains of light made out of bundled and woven optical fibers.

Lindy Roy in New York's meat-packing district, 2002.

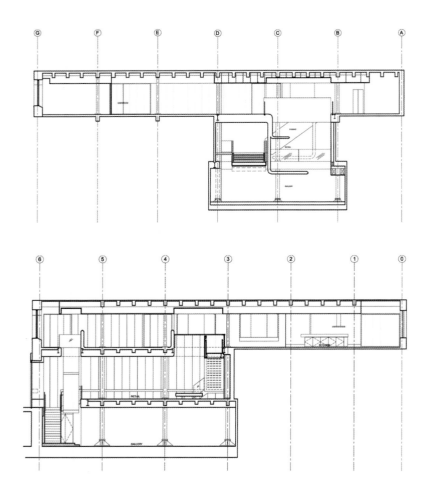

By moving its New York operations to Manhattan's meat-packing district while the area was still in transition, Vitra—true to form—was seeking to stake a claim for a new kind of environment to sell design. The brief asked us to rethink distinctions between gallery, retail, and contract showroom/office, and find ways to integrate those three aspects of Vitra culture. The gallery means research, an investment in ideas and innovation; the store is about accessibility, connection to the street; and the showroom and offices are the demonstration of products in daily use.

LINDY ROY, ON VITRA NEW YORK

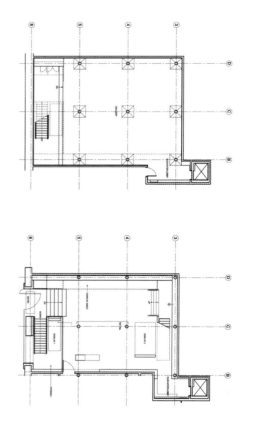

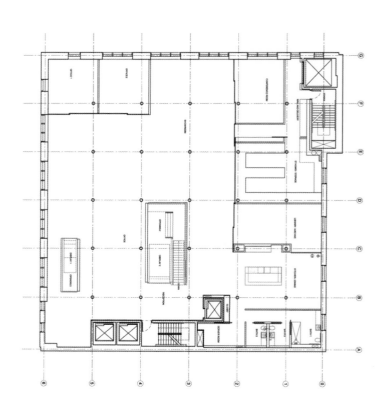

Vitra New York.

SANAA

The leaders of the next wave of Japanese avant-garde architecture, Kazuyo Sejima and Ryue Nishizawa of the Tokyo-based studio SANAA create buildings that are luminous and deceptively simple. With their delicate, veil-like glass exteriors that blur the line between public and private, the studio's projects have garnered considerable attention since its establishment in 1995.

SANAA first gained notice in the United States when its 1997 design for the M House was featured in the MoMA exhibition *The Unprivate House*. Created for maximum privacy in Tokyo, M House was built around a central courtyard that simultaneously provides light and seclusion from the public eye. For the design of the Christian Dior building on Tokyo's hip Omotesando Avenue—the largest Dior store in the world—Sejima looked to a gown from John Galliano's 1997 collection. The result was a tall, ethereal building that has become one of Japan's most notable new landmarks.

The studio's recent design for the New Museum of Contemporary Art in New York was praised for the way that it added to the site's context rather than merely adapting to it. A series of stacked levels, the museum tells the story of SoHo's history as an artist's community by architecturally evoking the open lofts that originally drew people to the neighborhood, while adding structural details that vividly point to the future.

The surrounding area is an upper-class district with large residences. However, density is increasing as lots in the area are being subdivided. This has created a situation of permanently drawn curtains and high fences. In this environment, we were faced with the question of how to bring the outside into the interior while at the same time securing the privacy of the space.

KAZUYO SEJIMA AND RYUE NISHIZAWA, ON THE M HOUSE

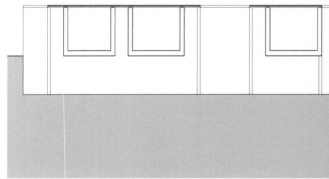

Kazuyo Sejima and Ryue Nishizawa at their studio in Shinagawa-ku, Tokyo, 2003.

The M House, Tokyo.

SHoP

The organizational chart of the young architecture firm SHoP looks like a family tree, formed as it is by a set of identical twin brothers, the wife of one of them, and another married couple. While none of them majored in architecture as undergraduates, the partners of SHoP/Sharples Holden Pasquarelli all met as architecture graduate students at Columbia University. The firm was established in 1996 when Christopher, William, and Coren Sharples joined with Kimberly Holden and Gregg Pasquarelli to work on a commission, and what was originally intended as a temporary arrangement turned into a permanent partnership.

SHoP has distinguished itself by using state-of-the-art computer technology borrowed from the film and animation industries to create unusual, undulating forms. The studio's first notable installation, *Dunescape*, was a temporary "urban beach" constructed of wood, vinyl, and water in the courtyard of MoMA/P.S. 1 in the summer of 2000. The studio's 2003 high-end condominium in New York's meat-packing district—cleverly called Porter House—is adding excitement to an already vibrant neighborhood. In March 2002, SHoP's luminous steel-and-light temporary bridge spanning Rector Street—the first project built at the Ground Zero site after the events of 9/11—opened to pedestrians, a sign of a return to normalcy for Lower Manhattan, and a symbol of architecture's potential power to heal. SHoP gained further notice with its design for the expansion of the Columbia University School of the Arts—that, when completed, will provide hybrid spaces for the school's increasingly cross-disciplinary environment.

Porter House represents an ongoing effort at SHoP to evolve a process of design that is less about style and more about technique. With the zinc skin of Porter House pixellated with a variety of heterogeneous materials, shapes, and sizes to create an identity for each of the apartments, SHoP is interested in creating a fluid practice rather than fluid form.

SHOP, ON PORTER HOUSE

Clockwise from left:
Coren Sharples, Kimberly Holden,
Gregg Pasquarelli, Christopher Sharples,
and William Sharples in a space
designed for Dakota Jackson, 2001.

The Porter House, New York.

ROBERT A.M. STERN

Best known for his shingled mansions and popular books on architectural history, Robert A. M. Stern has carved out a career for himself as a public spokesman for American architecture—even hosting an eight-part documentary series on architecture for PBS in 1986.

Stern's distinctly American eclecticism owes much to Robert Venturi, his mentor at Yale. After graduating in 1965, Stern reacted against modernism by adapting a vocabulary of traditional forms and motifs transformed by juxtaposition and humor, making him one of the country's first postmodern architects. After teaching architecture at Columbia University for many years, Stern opened up his own firm in New York. Stern's designs soon attracted the attention of the Walt Disney Company, a client also known for conflating traditional forms and entertainment. A member of Disney's board of directors from 1992 to 2003, Stern worked on a number of Disney projects, including a Feature Animation Building in Burbank, which boasts a mammoth version of Mickey's conical hat from *The Sorcerer's Apprentice*; a Colorado retreat for Disney CEO Michael Eisner; and the Disney Casting Center, an employee+training area near Orlando. But one of Stern's most comprehensive projects is Celebration, the Disney planned community on the outskirts of Walt Disney World. Some of Stern's other retro-historical projects include the 1993 Norman Rockwell Museum in the Berkshires, the 1994 tower addition to the Brooklyn Law School, and the 2003 Mark Twain Museum Center in Hartford. He has served as dean of the Yale School of Architecture since 1998.

The tower addition provides the 90-year-old school with expanded facilities and strengthens its image as an institution with a long history and a growing reputation. Located directly across from the recently renovated Brooklyn Borough Hall, our design visually establishes the law school as a component in the borough's traditional civic center.

ROBERT A.M. STERN, ON THE BROOKLYN LAW SCHOOL TOWER

FACADE DETAILS

THE BROOKLYN LAW SCHOOL TOWER
BROOKLYN, NEW YORK

The Brooklyn Law School Tower,
Brooklyn, New York.

BERNARD TSCHUMI

It can be said that some of the most important architects are not the ones who create monumental buildings and public spaces, but those who influence the generations to come through their teaching and theorizing. Bernard Tschumi has done both, as dean of Columbia's Graduate School of Architecture, Planning, and Preservation and as author of such books as *The Manhattan Transcripts, Architecture and Disjunction*, and *Event-Cities*.

After studying architecture in Paris and Zurich, Tschumi taught at various institutions in London and the United States before setting up a studio in Paris in 1983 to execute his winning design for Parc de la Villette, a 125-acre cultural facility on the outskirts of Paris. An urban ramble of buildings, gardens, bridges, and walkways, Parc de la Villette transformed the former site of Paris's slaughter-houses into a vibrantly planned public space. In the case of Le Fresnoy National Studio for Contemporary Arts in Tourcoing, France, Tschumi decided to create an immense overarching structure to protect the site's older buildings from the elements rather than raze them. His 2003 school of architecture for Florida International University uses brightly colored "generators" to ener-gize what might be an otherwise sober building. In a similar vein, the glass wall and soaring atrium that Tschumi designed for Alfred Lerner Hall at Columbia University dramatizes the move-ment of the students who use the space's ramps, and plays up the tension between the campus's nineteenth-century master plan and Tschumi's contrasting style and material.

Bernard Tschumi in his New York studio, 2002.

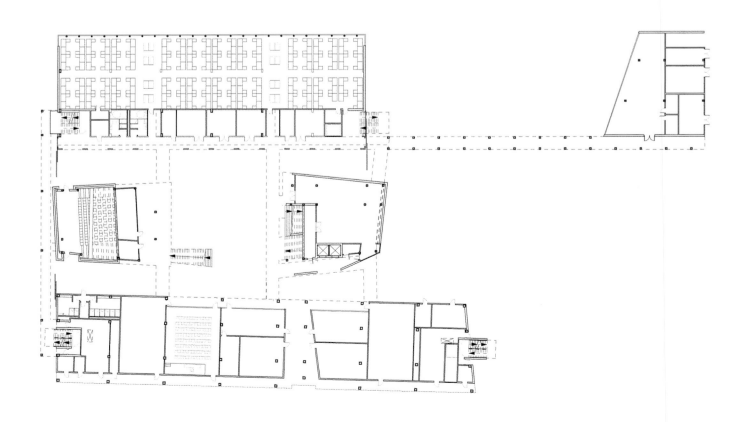

The School of Architecture at Florida International University, Miami.

The key for a new school is its ability to set a stage and scene that define a cultural identity. A new building must contribute to making that scene and identity. Here, what the building does is as important as what it looks like. The building must act as a generator, activating spaces as well as defining them. Our project consists of two sober wings that define a space activated by exuberantly colorful generators.

BERNARD TSCHUMI, ON THE SCHOOL OF ARCHITECTURE AT FLORIDA INTERNATIONAL UNIVERSITY

ROBERT VENTURI
DENISE SCOTT BROWN

"Less is a bore," Robert Venturi famously declared at the start of his 1966 book *Complexity and Contradiction in Architecture*, playing off of Mies van der Rohe's famous minimalist dictum. With that tome and the 1972 *Learning from Las Vegas*, Venturi and his wife, Denise Scott Brown, laid the theoretical groundwork for post-modern architecture.

After getting his MFA from Princeton University in 1950, spending two years in Italy as a Rome Prize Fellow, and working in the studios of Louis Kahn and Eero Saarinen, Robert Venturi established Venturi and Rauch with colleague John Rauch. In 1967 the African-born Scott Brown, known for her expertise in urban planning and design, joined the practice. The partnership soon cemented its reputation for exuberant buildings that often reference historic styles in ironic ways, such as Franklin Court, a museum and memorial to Benjamin Franklin in Venturi's hometown, Philadelphia; the Allen Memorial Art Museum at Oberlin College; the BASCO Showroom in Philadelphia; and the Lewis Thomas Laboratory for Molecular Biology at Princeton University.

In 1989, Venturi Scott Brown & Associates was founded, and in 1991 the firm's addition to London's National Gallery—the Sainsbury Wing—opened to great acclaim. Recent works have ranged from the Seattle Art Museum to the University of Pennsylvania's Perelman Quadrangle to the Mielparque Nikko Kirifuri Resort near Nikko, Japan. In 1991 Venturi was the recipient of the prestigious Pritzker Architecture Prize, and in 1997 Scott Brown was awarded the AIA Topaz Award for excellence in architectural education.

Denise Scott Brown and Robert Venturi
at their studio in Philadelphia, 1999.

A building designed to work inside and out—with gallery space appropriate as recessive background to accommodate a specific collection of paintings in gentle light—and an exterior both historically symbolic and modernist to accommodate its varying important contexts—acknowledging the historical National Gallery building as it inflects toward Trafalgar Square, Pall Mall East, and back streets.

ROBERT VENTURI AND DENISE SCOTT BROWN, ON THE SAINSBURY WING OF THE NATIONAL GALLERY

CLIPPER CLASS

Welcome Aboard Pan Am's
Special Business Class

Libations

Aperitifs	Cocktails	Spirits	Red and White Wines
Sparkling Wine	Premium Beer		Liqueurs and Cognac

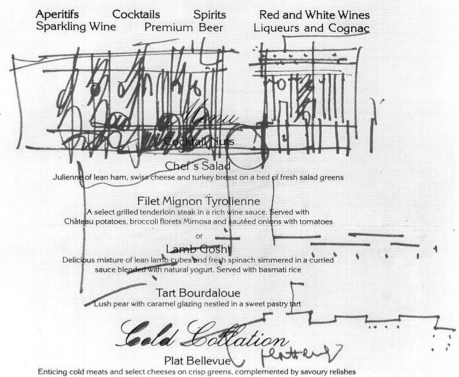

Menu

Cocktail Nuts

Chef's Salad
Julienne of lean ham, swiss cheese and turkey breast on a bed of fresh salad greens

Filet Mignon Tyrolienne
A select grilled tenderloin steak in a rich wine sauce. Served with
Château potatoes, broccoli florets Mimosa and sautéed onions with tomatoes

or

Lamb Gosht
Delicious mixture of lean lamb cubes and fresh spinach simmered in a curried
sauce blended with natural yogurt. Served with basmati rice

Tart Bourdaloue
Lush pear with caramel glazing nestled in a sweet pastry tart

Cold Collation

Plat Bellevue
Enticing cold meats and select cheeses on crisp greens, complemented by savoury relishes

Bakery Fresh Roll and Creamery Butter

Apple Strudel

Coffee	Taster's Choice Decaffeinated Coffee	Tea
Coca-Cola	Tab	Diet Coke	Canada Dry Beverages

Country Time® Lemonade Flavor Drink

530C
9-17-84

Please accept our apology if your choice of entree is not available.

91

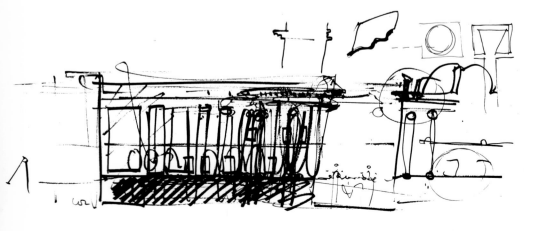

The Sainsbury Wing of the National Gallery of Art, London.

RAFAEL VIÑOLY

Born in Uruguay in 1944 to a theater director and a math teacher, Rafael Viñoly moved to Argentina when he was 4. Although he originally intended to be a concert pianist, he soon switched to architecture, which he saw as a more "stable" profession. Viñoly won his first architectural competition at age 18, the same year he entered the School of Architecture at the University of Buenos Aires. By 20, Viñoly had established his own practice, Estudio de Arquitectura, which went on to become one of Latin America's largest and most influential design studios. The brutality of Argentina's military regime, however, compelled Viñoly to relocate to the United States in 1978, where he spent a brief period as guest lecturer at the Harvard University Graduate School of Design. He then settled permanently in New York and founded Rafael Viñoly Architects PC.

Viñoly's first major project in New York was the John Jay College of Criminal Justice, which established his reputation as an artful designer of public-sector projects. But it was his elegant plan for the Tokyo International Forum that elevated Viñoly to world prominence: the proposal's ship-reminiscent glass and steel structure beat out 394 architects for the 1989 commission. This success led to other notable public projects, including the 1998 Princeton University Stadium, the 2001 Kimmel Center for the Performing Arts in Philadelphia, and the proposed expansion for the John F. Kennedy Center for the Performing Arts. As part of the THINK team—which included fellow architects Shigeru Ban, Frederic Schwartz, and Ken Smith—Viñoly became a finalist for the World Trade Center commission with a plan for two soaring Towers of Culture that would be built above and around the previous buildings' footprints.

Located on Philadelphia's Avenue of the Arts, just a few blocks from City Hall, the Kimmel Center for the Performing Arts evokes the image of two jewels in a glass case.

RAFAEL VIÑOLY, ON THE KIMMEL CENTER

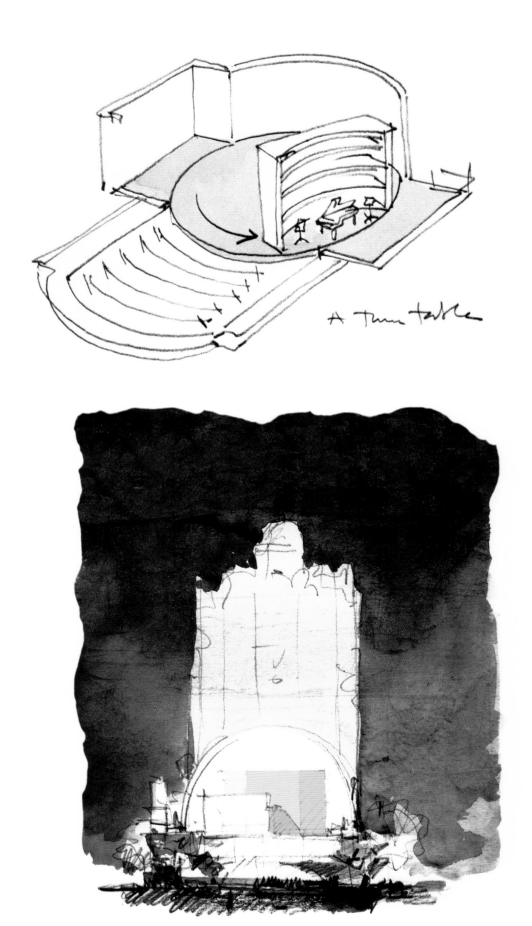

A Turn table

The Kimmel Center for the Performing Arts, Philadelphia.

TOD WILLIAMS
BILLIE TSIEN

One of the biggest challenges facing Tod Williams and Billie Tsien when designing the 2001 American Folk Art Museum on West 53rd Street in New York was the size of the diminutive lot: 30,000 square feet. Another was how to create a structure that would hold its own against the cultural behemoth down the block, the Museum of Modern Art. The partners' solution was to create an eight-story building that maximizes light in order to create inviting spaces for the museum's collections. The building's façade, made from a honey-colored silicon and bronze alloy that looks handcrafted, provides an appropriately idiosyncratic entrance to an institution that specializes in folk artifacts.

The husband-and-wife team has become known for experimenting with new materials such as Homasote, plastic laminates, expanded metal mesh, and resins, causing them to earn the reputation of being tactile architects whose work distinctly bridges the visceral and the cerebral. That many of their projects involve the arts is not surprising given that during the years Williams worked for Richard Meier in the late 1960s and early '70s, Tsien was studying fine art at Yale and painting fulltime.

In 1986, several years after Tsien completed her architectural studies at UCLA, the couple became business partners and opened a New York office. Since then, their studio has completed numerous institutional commissions in the United States, including the Phoenix Art Museum and the Neurosciences Institute in La Jolla, as well as a pool house on Long Island with a seventy-foot mural by Sol Lewitt.

Tod Williams and Billie Tsien
inside the American Folk Art Museum, 2001.

Folk Art is art created by untrained artists. Work comes not so much from the head, but rather more directly from the heart to the hand. We wanted to design a museum that would have the same kind of idiosyncratic and personal nature that folk art possesses.

TOD WILLIAMS AND BILLIE TSIEN, ON THE AMERICAN FOLK ART MUSEUM

American Folk Art Museum, New York.

PETER ZUMTHOR

Peter Zumthor believes in the experience of architecture rather than in the theory of it. For Zumthor, once a building exists in a place it must be visited in order to be understood. Straightforward and elusive at the same time, Zumthor's work—which is often situated in mountainous areas—has an almost mystical quality to it that softens his otherwise minimalist tendencies.

Born in Basel in 1954, Zumthor was trained as a cabinetmaker before studying architecture at the Kunstgewerbeschule Basel and the Pratt Institute in Brooklyn. After establishing his architecture studio in 1979, Zumthor developed his hallmark humane minimalism on public and private projects throughout Switzerland, including his own studio, which he built in 1986. His Church of Saint Benedict from 1989 is based on a highly complex geometric structure that is both sensuous and dynamic. And his highly praised Thermal Baths in Vals—named a "protected building" only two years after completion—respectfully complements the remote Alpine village in which it is situated. By suggesting a huge rock embedded in the side of the mountain, what could easily have been an austere modernist block is instead a sensual, ethereal site of experience that was inspired by images of quarries and flowing water.

Similarly, Zumthor's Art Museum in Bregenz, Austria, is completely suited to its location on the shore of Lake Constance. Essentially a cube, the museum is encased in large panels of finely etched glass specially designed to catch light and make the building look alternatively like a lantern or an extension of the mist that hovers over the surface of the lake.

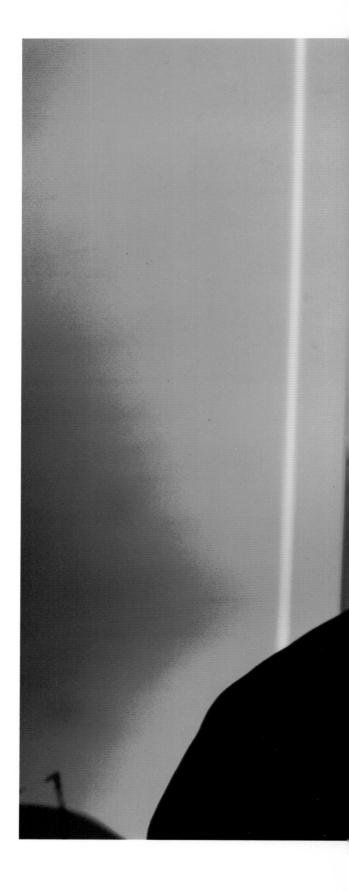

Peter Zumthor outside his studio in Switzerland, 2003.

There is a magical power in every completed, self-contained creation, in every fully developed architectural structure. It is perhaps only when the building is complete that we notice the small elements, and our attention is caught by a detail such as two nails in the floor that hold the steel plates by the worn-out doorstep. Emotions well up. Something moves us.

PETER ZUMTHOR, ON ARCHITECTURE

MAJOR PROJECTS

RAIMUND ABRAHAM: House Dapra, *Salzburg, Austria;* Hause Pless, *Vienna, Austria;* House Woolner, *Connecticut;* House M. Dellacher, *Oberwart, Austria;* Low-Income Housing, *Providence, Rhode Island;* M.A.Z.E.-Experimental Daycare Center; Rainbow Plaza, *Niagra Falls, New York;* House Bernard, *Tyrol, Austria;* Anthology Film Archives, *New York, New York;* Siedlung Traviatagasse, *Vienna, Austria;* Monument for the Cooper Union, *New York, New York;* Residential and Commercial Building, *Graz, Austria;* Hypo-House, *Tyrol, Austria;* and the Austrian Cultural Forum, *New York, New York.*

TADAO ANDO: Row House, Sumiyoshi, Japan; Rokko Housing I, *Kobe, Japan;* Time's I, *Kyoto, Japan;* Church of the Light, *Osaka, Japan;* Museum of Literature, *Himeji, Japan;* Water Temple, *Awaji Island, Japan;* Japan Pavilion Expo '92, *Sevilla, Spain;* Naoshima Contemporary Art Museum & Annex, *Okayama, Japan;* Gallery for Japanese Screen, the Art Institute of Chicago, *Chicago, Illinois;* Rokko Housing II, *Kobe, Japan;* Chikatsu-Asuka Historical Museum, *Osaka, Japan;* Meditation Space, UNESCO, *Paris, France;* House in Chicago, *Chicago, Illinois;* TOTO Seminar House, *Tsuna-gun, Japan;* Daylight Museum (Hiroki Oda Museum), *Gamo-gun, Japan;* Rokko Housing III, *Kobe, Japan;* Awaji-Yumebutai (Awaji Island Project), *Tsuna-gun, Japan;* Komyo-ji Temple, *Saijo, Japan;* FABRICA (Benneton Communications Research Center), *Treviso, Italy;* Pulitzer Foundation for the Arts, *St. Louis, Missouri;* ARMANI/TEATRO, *Milan, Italy;* Sayamaike Historical Museum, *Osaka, Japan;* Shiba Ryotaro Memorial Museum, *Osaka, Japan;* Hyogo Prefectural Museum of Art, *Kobe, Japan;* The International Library of Children's Literature, *Tokyo, Japan;* Piccadilly Gardens Regeneration, *Manchester, England;* and the Modern Art Museum of Fort Worth, *Fort Worth, Texas.*

ARQUITECTONICA: Pink House, *Miami, Florida;* Palace, *Miami, Florida;* Atlantis, *Miami, Florida;* Banco de Credito, *Lima, Peru;* Center for Innovative Technology, *Washington, DC.;* U.S. Embassy, *Lima, Peru;* Banque de Luxembourg, *Luxembourg;* Festival Walk, *Hong Kong, China;* Westin Hotel Time Square, *New York, New York;* Shanghai Info Town, *Shanghai, China;* Philips Arena, *Atlanta, Georgia;* Nexus World, *Fukuoka, Japan;* American Airlines Arena, *Miami, Florida;* Dijon Performing Arts Center, *Dijon, France;* Miami City Ballet, *Miami, Florida;* Pacific Plaza Towers, *Manila, Phillipines;* Cyberport Technology Campus, *Hong Kong, China;* Aventura Government Center, *Aventura, Florida;* Miami Children's Museum, *Miami, Florida;* Bank of America/BMG Offices, *Beverly Hills, California;* Discovery Science Center, *Santa Ana, California;* Miranova Residential & Office Towers, *Columbus, Ohio;* Lima Marriott Hotel & Office Tower, *Lima, Peru;* and Waverly at South Beach, *Miami Beach, Florida.*

SHIGERU BAN: "Alvar Aalto" Exhibition design for the Axis Gallery, *Tokyo, Japan;* House with Double Roof, Lake Yamanaka, *Yamanashi, Japan;* Issey Miyake Gallery, *Tokyo, Japan;* Furniture House, Lake Yamanaka, *Yamanashi, Japan;* Curtain Wall House, *Tokyo, Japan;* Paper House, Lake Yamanaka, Yamanashi; Paper Church, *Kobe, Hyogo, Japan;* 2/5 House, Nishinomiya, *Japan;* Wall-less House, Karuizawa, *Nagano, Japan;* 9 Square Grid House, *Kanagawa, Japan;* Paper Arch installation in the MoMA Sculpture Garden, *New York, New York;* Naked House, *Kawagoe, Japan;* Picture Window House, *Izu, Shizuoka, Japan;* and the Glass Shutter House, *Tokyo, Japan.*

DEBORAH BERKE: Battery Park City Parks Conservancy, *New York, New York;* Hope Branch Library, *Columbus, Indiana;* Marlboro College Master Plan, *Marlboro, Vermont;* the Yale School of Art and New Theater, *New Haven, Connecticut;* and Temple University: Tyler School of Art Planning & Design Study, *Philadelphia, Pennsylvania.*

SANTIAGO CALATRAVA: Bach de Roda Bridge, *Barcelona, Spain;* the Alamillo Bridge and viaduct, *Seville, Spain;* Campo Volantin Footbridge in *Bilbao, Spain;* Alameda Bridge and underground station in *Valencia;* BCE Place Hall in *Toronto;* Lyon Airport Station, *Lyon-Satolas, France;* Oriente railway station, *Lisbon, Portugal;* Sondica Airport, *Bilbao, Spain;* The Bridge of Europe, *Orléans, France;* the Bodegas Ysios winery *in Laguardia, Spain;* expansion of the Milwaukee Art Museum, *Milwaukee, Wisconsin;* James Joyce Bridge, *Dublin Ireland,* and the Auditorio de Tenerife, *Santa Cruz, Canary Islands, Spain.*
Awards: designation as a Global Leader for Tomorrow *by the World Economic Forum in Davos, Switzerland;* the Creu Sant Jordi, *Barcelona, Spain;* the Gold Medal for Merit *in the Fine Arts, Ministry of Culture, Spain;* membership in Les Arts et Lettres,

Paris, France; Time Magazine's *"Best of 2001"* designation for the expansion of the Milwaukee Art Museum; the Sir Misha Black Medal, *Royal College of Art, London, United Kingdom;* the Leonardo da Vinci Medal, *Florence, Italy;* Société pour la Formation des Ingénieurs and the Principe de Asturias Art Prize, *Oviedo, Spain;* and the Gold Medal of Architecture of *L'Académie d'Architecture, Paris, France.* In 1968 Santiago Calatrava enrolled in the Escuela Tecnica Superior de Arquitectura, where he earned a degree in architecture and took a post-graduate course in urbanism. He then pursued post-graduate studies at the ETH (Federal Institute of Technology) in Zurich, receiving his Ph.D. in 1979.

DAVID CHILDS: Washington Mall master plan and Constitution Gardens; the National Geographic headquarters building, *Washington, DC.;* 1300 New York Avenue; Metro Center, *Washington, DC.;* the U.S. News and World Report headquarters, *Washington, DC.;* the Evening Star renovation and addition on Pennsylvania Avenue, *Washington, DC.;* the Four Seasons Hotel, *Washington, DC.;* Regent Hotel, *Washington, DC.;* Park Hyatt Hotel, *Washington, DC.;* expansion of the Dulles Airport main terminal, *Washington, DC.;.* Worldwide Plaza, *New York, New York;* 450 Lexington Avenue *New York, New York;* Bertelsmann Tower at Times Square, *New York;* the New York Mercantile Exchange, *New York, New York;* JFK International Arrivals Building, *New York, New York;* Bear Sterns Headquarters, *New York, New York;* master plan for Rivrside South, *New York, New York;* Stuyvesant School Bridge, *New York, New York;* renovation and preservation of Lever House, *New York, New York;* Time Warner Center, *New York, New York;* Swiss Bank Center, *Stamford, Connecticut;* U.S. Courthouse, *Charleston, West Virginia;* Lester B. Pearson International Airport, *Toronto, Canada;* the Ben Gurion International Airport, *Tel Aviv, Isreal;* West Ferry Circus at Canary Wharf, *London, England;* and the United States Embassy in *Ottowa, Canada.*

HENRY COBB: Royal Bank of Canada Building at Place Ville Marie, *Montreal, Canada;* Campus of the State University College at Fredonia, *New York;* John Hancock Tower, *Boston, Massachusetts;* World Trade Center, *Baltimore, Maryland;* Collins Place, *Melbourne, Australia;* 16th Street Transitway Mall, *Denver, Colorado;* Johnson & Johnson World Headquarters, *New Brunswick, New Jersey;* Mobil Research Laboratory, *Farmers Branch, Texas;* Arco Tower, *Dallas, Texas;* Portland Museum of Art, *Portland, Maine;* Pitney-Bowes World Headquarters, *Stamford, Connecticut;* Fountain Place, *Dallas, Texas;* Columbia Square, *Washington, DC.;* Commerce Square, *Philadelphia, Pennsylvania;* Library Tower, *Los Angeles, California;* Headquarters of Credit Suisse First Boston at Canary Wharf, *London, England;* Anderson Graduate School of Management at the University of California, *Los Angeles, Califronia;* the Headquarters of the American Association for the Advancement of Science, *Washington, DC.;* John Moakley United States Courthouse and Harborpark, *Boston, Massachusetts;* Head Office of ABN AMRO Bank, *Amsterdam, The Netherlands;* China Europe International Business School, *Shanghai, China;* College-Conservatory of Music at the University of Cincinnati, *Cincinnati, Ohio;* 2099 Pennsylvania Avenue, *Washington, DC.;* Friend Center for Engineering Education at Princeton University, *Princeton, New Jersey;* Tour EDF at La Défense, *Paris, France;* United States Courthouse, *Hammond, Indiana;* World Trade Center and Grand Marina Hotel, *Barcelona;* POS Plaza, *Shanghai, China;* and the National Constitution Center, *Philadelphia, Pennsylvania.*

ELIZABETH DILLER AND RICARDO SCOFIDIO: the Brasserie restaurant in the Seagram Building, *New York, New York;* Travelogues, a permanent installation at the new JFK International Arrivals Terminal, *New York, New York;* Master/Slave, an installation at the Fondation Cartier, *Paris, France;* Slither, 104 units of social housing, *Gifu, Japan;* EJM1: Man Walking at Ordinary Speed and EJM2: Inertia, two dance collaborations with the Lyon Ballet Opera and Charleroi Danses; Refresh, a web project for the Dia Art Foundation; The American Lawn: Surface of Everyday Life, an exhibition at the Canadian Centre for Architecture in *Montreal;* InterClone Hotel, an installation at the Ataturk Airport for the Istanbul Biennial; and Pageant, a video installation for the Johannesburg Biennial; X,Y, a permanent installation for a pachinko parlor, *Kobe, Japan;* Jump Cuts, a permanent video marquee for the world's largest Cineplex theater, *San Jose, California;* Moving Target, a collaborative dance work with Charleroi/Danses *Belgium;* Business Class, a collaborative theater work with Dumb Type and Hotel Pro Forma for Copenhagen Cultural Capital; Indigestion, an interactive video installation; Subtopia, an electronic project for the ICC Gallery in *Tokyo*; Blur Building; a media pavilion for Swiss EXPO 2002; a master plan for Brooklyn Academy of Music Cultural District for BAMLDC in collaboration with Rem Koolhaas; and the Viewing Platform for Ground Zero at the World Trade Center site, *New York, New York*.

WINKA DUBBELDAM: Mixed-Media Art Gallery, *New York, New York*; NOHO Loft, *New York, New York*; Residence in Millbrook, *Millbrook, New York*; Wooster Street Loft, *New York, New York*; Gear Magazine offices, *New York, New York*; Urban Design Maashaven, *Rotterdam, The Netherlands*; Urban Design for Moscow & proposal for an office tower; New Museum for the Eniac, *Philadelphia, Pennsylvania*; Restaurant in Scheveningen, *The Netherlands*; BitForms, *New York, New York*; Gipsy Trail Residence, *Kent, New York*; Greenwich Street Building, *New York, New York*; Maashaven Towers, *Rotterdam, The Netherlands*; Urban Scheme for Schoonhoven, *The Netherlands*; Eco Resort, *Shepherds Island, Panama*; and the Museum for Contemporary Design, *Schoonhoven, The Netherlands*.

PETER EISENMAN: Wexner Center for the Visual Arts, *Columbus, Ohio*; Fine Arts Library at the Ohio State University, *Columbus, Ohio*; Koizumi Sangyo Corporation headquarters building, *Tokyo, Japan*; social housing at Checkpoint Charlie, along the Berlin Wall, *Berlin, Germany*; Greater Columbus Convention Center, *Columbus, Ohio*; and the Aronoff Center for Design and Art at the University of *Cincinnati*.

LORD FOSTER: Willis Faber & Dumas Head Office, *Ipswich, England*; Sainsbury Centre for Visual Arts, *Norwich, England*; Hongkong and Shanghai Bank, *Hong Kong*; Sackler Galleries at the Royal Academy, *London, England*; Stansted Airport, *London, England*; Century Tower, *Tokyo, Japan*; Carré d'Art, *Nîmes, France*; Commerzbank Headquarters, *Frankfurt, Germany*; American Air Museum, *Duxford, England*; Hong Kong International Airport; German Parliament at the Reichstag, *Berlin, Germany*; the Great Court at the British Museum, *London, England*; and the Millennium Bridge, *London*.
Recent projects: the Center for Clinical Science Research and the James H. Clark Center at Stanford University, *Stanford, California*; the transformation of Trafalgar Square in *London, England*; new City Academy Schools in *Brent* and *Bexley, England*; the McLaren Technology Centre, *Surrey, England*; Hearst Headquarters in *New York, New York*; an office tower and a residential development in *Sydney, Australia*; the Museum of Fine Arts, *Boston, Massachusetts*; a new terminal for Beijing Capital International Airport, *China*; a city quarter in *Milan, Italy*; and an Opera House in *Dallas, Texas*.

JAMES INGO FREED: 88 Pine Street, *New York, New York*; National Bank of Commerce in *Lincoln, Nebraska*; One West Loop Plaza in *Houston, Texas*; Gem City Savings in *Dayton, Ohio*; 499 Park Avenue, *New York, New York*; Warwick Post Oak Hotel in *Houston, Texas*; Jacob K. Javits Convention Center and Plaza in *New York City*; Potomac Tower, *Rosslyn, Virginia*; the 57-story First Bank Place in *Minneapolis, Minnesota*; United States Holocaust Memorial Museum, *Washington, D.C.*; the expansion and modernization of the Los Angeles Convention Center, *Los Angeles, California*; the San Francisco Main Public Library at the Civic Center, *San Francisco, California*; the Ronald Reagan Building and International Trade Center, *Washington, D.C.*; the four-building Science and Engineering Quad at Stanford University, *Palo Alto, California*; the Roman L. Hruska United States Courthouse in *Omaha, Nebraska*; and the Broad Center for the Biological *Sciences at California Institute of Technology, Pasadena, California*.

FRANK GEHRY: Guggenheim Museum Bilbao, *Bilbao, Spain*; DZ Bank Building, *Berlin, Germany*; Experience Music Project, *Seattle, Washington*; Ohr-O'Keefe Museum, *Biloxi, Mississippi*; Bard College Performing Arts Center, *Annandale-on-Hudson, New York*; Millennium Park Music Pavilion and Great Lawn, *Chicago, Illinois*; Corcoran Gallery and School of Art, *Washington, D.C.*; Team Disneyland Administration Building, *Anaheim, California*; Nationale-Nederlanden Building, *Prague, Czech Republic*; Walt Disney Concert Hall, *Los Angeles, California*; Chiat/Day Office Building, *Venice, California*; Vitra International Furniture Museum and Factory, *Weil am Rhein, Germany*; and the Vitra International Headquarters, *Basel, Switzerland*.

MICHAEL GRAVES: Humana Building, *Louisville, Kentucky*; Team Disney headquarters, *Burbank, California*; the Walt Disney World Swan and Dolphin

Hotels, *Orlando, Florida*; Denver Central Library, *Denver, Colorado*; Newark Museum, *Newark, New Jersey*; International Finance Corporation, *Washington, DC*; Headquarters for the Ministry of Health and Sport, The Hague, The Netherlands; Federal Bank of Dallas, *Houston, Texas*; Headquarters for the Department of Transportation, *Washington, D.C.*; and the United States Federal Courthouse, *Washington, D.C.*

CHARLES GWATHMEY: Gwathmey Residence and Studio, *Amagansett, New York*; Princeton University, Whig Hall, *Princeton, New Jersey*; Thomas & Betts Corporation Office Building; Lincoln Center for the Performing Arts: Retail Concourse and Administrative Offices, *New York, New York*; Evans Partnership Office Building, *Parsipanny, New Jersey*; Triangle Pacific Corporation Office Building, *Dallas, Texas*; Beverly Hills Civic Center, *Beverly Hills, California*; Westover School Library and Science Building, *Middlebury, Connecticut*; University of Nebraska Wick Alumni Center, *Lincoln, Nebraska*; American Museum of the Moving Image, *Astoria, New York*; University of North Carolina Thomas I. Storrs College of Architecture Building, *Charlotte, North Carolina*; Morgan Stanley Dean Witter and Co. World Headquarters, *New York, New York*; Harvard University: Werner Otto Hall, Busch-Reisinger Museum/Fine Arts Library, Addition to the Fogg Museum, *Cambridge, Massachusetts*; Solomon R. Guggenheim Museum: Renovation and Addition, *New York, New York*; SONY Enterntainment, Inc. World Headquarter, *New York, New York*; The New York Public Library: The Science, Industry, and Business Library (SIBL), *New York, New York*; Citicorp Center: Tower, Plaza, and Retail Atrium, *New York, New York*; Princeton University: James S. Mc Donnell Hall of Physics, *Princeton, New Jersey*; Solomon R. Guggenheim Museum: The Sackler Center for Arts Education, *New York, New York*; International Center of Photography, *New York, New York*; and the Middlebury College Library, *Middlebury, Vermont*.

ZAHA HADID: Vitra Fire Station and the Lfone Pavilion, Weil am Rhein, Germany; housing project for IBA-Block 2, *Berlin, Germany*; Mind Zone at the Millennium Dome, *London, England*; Tram Station and Car Park, *Strasbourg, France*; Ski Jump, *Innsbruck, Austria*; and Contemporary Arts Center, *Cincinnati, Ohio*.

JACQUES HERZOG AND PIERRE DE MEURON: Blue House, Oberwil, Switzerland; the Ricola Storage Building, *Laufen, Switzerland*; the Stone House, *Tavole, Italy*; the Apartment Building along a Party Wall, *Basel, Switzerland*; The Goetz Collection, *Munich, Germany*; Dominus Winery, *Yountville, California*; Eberswalde Technical School Library, *Eberswalde, Germany*; Tate Modern, London, England; Laban Dance Center, *London, England*; and Prada Aoyama Tokyo, *Tokyo, Japan*.

STEVEN HOLL: American Memorial Library, *Berlin, Germany*; D.E. Shaw & Co. Offices, *New York, New York*; Knut Hamsun Museum, *Hamarøy, Norway*; University of California at San Francisco, Mission Bay Campus, *San Francisco, California*; Pratt Institute, Higgins Hall, *Brooklyn, New York*; Chapel of St. Ignatius, *Seattle, Washington*; Museum of Contemporary Art, *Helsinki, Finland*; Cranbrook Institute of Science, *Bloomfield Hills, Michigan*; Whitney Waterworks Park, *Hamden, Connecticut*; Masterplan, M.I.T. Vassar Street, *Cambridge, Massachusetts*; University of Iowa, *Iowa City, Iowa*; Nelson Atkins Museum of Art, *Kansas City, Missouri*; Sarphatistraat Offices, *Amsterdam, The Netherlands*; Loisium Visitor Center, *Langelois, Austria*; Musee des confluences, *Lyon France*; Bellevue Art Museum, *Bellevue, Washington*; Foundation Pinault Ile Seguin, *Paris, France*; College of Architecture and Landscape Architecture, *Minneapolis, Minnesota*; Simmons Hall, Massachusetts Institute of Technology, *Cambridge, Massachusetts*; Toolenburg-Zuid, *Schipol, The Netherlands*; Green Urban Laboratory, *Nanning, China*; Beirut Marina, Apartments & Public Space, *Beirut, Lebanon*.

HANS HOLLEIN: Retti Candleshop, *Vienna, Austria*; Municipal Museum Abteiberg Moenchengladbach, *Germany*; Museum of Glass and Ceramics, *Tehran, Iran*; Museum of Modern Art, *Frankfurt am Main, Germany*; Haas-Haus, *Vienna, Austria*; Banco Santander, *Madrid, Spain*; General Media Tower, *Vienna, Austria*; Headquarter of the Interbank, *Lima, Peru*; Austrian Embassy, *Berlin, Germany*; "Vulcania" (Museum of Vulcanism), *Auvergne, France*; Centrum Bank, *Vaduz, Liechtenstein*; Albertina Museum, Entrance and Front Area, *Vienna, Austria*; and San Giovanni Valdarno Masterplan and Buildings, *Italy*.

ARATA ISOZAKI: Oita Medical Hall and Annex, *Oita, Japan;* Oita Prefectural Library, *Oita, Japan;* Expo '70-Festival Plaza, *Osaka, Japan;* The Museum of Modern Art, *Gunma, Japan;* Tsukuba Center Building, *Ibaragi, Japan;* The Museum of Contemporary Art, *Los Angeles, California;* Palau D'Esports Sant Jordi, *Barcelona, Spain;* Art Tower Mito, *Ibaragi, Japan;* Team Disney Building, *Florida;* The Center of Japanese Art and Technology, *Kraków, Poland;* Nagi Museum of Contemporary Art, *Okayama, Japan;* Kyoto Concert Hall, *Kyoto, Japan;* Nara Centennial Hall, *Nara, Japan;* DOMUS: La Casa del Hombre (Interactive Museum about Humans), *La Caruña, Spain;* Okayama West Police Station, *Okayama, Japan;* Shizuoka Convention & Arts Center, *Shizuoka, Japan;* The Akiyoshidai International Arts Village; COSI-Ohio's Center of Science & Industry, Ohio; Ceramics Park MINO, *Gifu, Japan;* and Project for New Gate to Cultural de la Caixa, *Barcelona, Spain.*

TOYO ITO: Aluminum House, *Kanagawa, Japan;* House in Nakano, "White U," *Tokyo, Japan;* Silver Hut, house of the architect, *Tokyo, Japan;* Tower of Winds in Yokohama, *Kanagawa, Japan;* Guest House for Sapporo Beer Brewery, *Hokkaido, Japan;* Yatsushiro Municipal Museum, *Kumamoto, Japan;* Shimosuwa Municipal Museum, *Nagano, Japan;* Old People's Home in Yatsushiro, *Kumamoto, Japan;* Yatsushiro Fire Station, *Kumamoto, Japan;* Nagaoka Lyric Hall, *Niigata, Japan;* Community Activities and Senior Citizens' Day Care Center in Yokohama, *Kanagawa, Japan;* Dome in Odate, *Akita, Japan;* Notsuharu Town Hall, *Oita, Japan;* T Hall in Taisha, *Shimane, Japan;* Agriculture Park, *Oita, Japan;* Health Future Pavilion at Expo 2000, *Hannover, Germany;* Sendai Mediatheque, *Miyagi, Japan;* Brugge 2002 Pavilion, *Brugge, Belgium;* and the Serpentine Gallery Pavilion (2002).

PHILIP JOHNSON: Glass House, *New Canaan, Connecticut;* Rockefeller Guest House, *New York, New York;* Sheldon Memorial Art Gallery at the University of Nebraska, *Lincoln, Nebraska;* the New York State Theater at Lincoln Center, *New York, New York;* addition to the Museum of Modern Art, *New York, New York;* the New York State Pavilion at the World's Fair, *New York, New York;* Pannzoil Place, *Houston, Texas;* AT&T Building, *New York, New York;* Republic Bank Center, *Houston, Texas;* Transco Tower, *Houston, Texas;* PPG Place, *Pittsburgh, Pennsylvania;* Momentum Place, *Dallas, Texas;* and Museum of Television and Radio, *New York, New York.*

REM KOOLHAAS: Netherlands Dance Theatre, *The Hague, The Netherlands;* Nexus Housing, *Fukuoka, Japan;* Villa dall'Ava, *Paris, France;* Kunsthal, *Rotterdam, The Netherlands;* Euralille Masterplan, *Lille, France;* Lille Grand Palais, *Lille, France;* Educatorium, *Utrect, the Netherlands;* Maison à Bordeaux, *France;* Guggenheim Hermitage, *Las Vegas, Nevada;* Guggenheim Museum, *Las Vegas, Nevada;* Prada Epicenter Store, *New York, New York;* Performance Centre 't Paard van Troje, *The Hague, The Netherlands;* Illinois Institute of Technology Campus Center, *Chicago, Illinois;* and the Netherlands Embassy, *Berlin, Germany.*

RICARDO LEGORRETA: Camino Real Hotel; an office building for IBM; the Camino Real Hotel in *Cancun;* the Kodak Laboratories Building; a factory for Renault, in Gomez Palacio, *Durango, Mexico;* Camino Real Ixtapa Hotel; the Master Plan for the City of Jurica, Queretaro; Solana Westlake-Southlake in *Dallas, Texas;* Club Mediterraneé in Huatulco, *Oaxaca, Mexico;* Westin Regina Hotel in Cancun, *Quintana Roo, Mexico;* the Children's Discovery Museum in *San Jose, California;* the Contemporary Art Museum (MARCO) in *Monterrey, Nuevo Leon, Mexico;* the Papalote Children's Museum in *Mexico City;* the Tech Museum of Innovation in *San Jose, California;* and the Metropolitan Cathedral of *Managua in Nicaragua.*

DANIEL LIBESKIND: the Osaka Folly, *Osaka, Japan;* Making the City Boundaries, *Groningen, The Netherlands;* Polderland Garden, *Almere, The Netherlands;* Uozo Mountain Pavilion, *Uozo, Japan;* Serpentine Pavilion, Serpentine Gallery, *London, England;* the Felix Nussbaum Museum, *Osnabrück, Germany;* The Jewish Museum, *Berlin, Germany;* Imperial War Museum North, *Manchester, England;* The Weil Gallery, *Mallorca, Spain;* and the London Metropolitan University Graduate School, *London, England.*

GREG LYNN: Stranded Sears Tower, *Chicago, Illinois;* Cabrini Green Urban Design Competition, *Chicago, Illinois;* Citron House, *Amagansett, New York;* H2 House Visitors Pavilion and Information Center, *Schwechat, Austria;* the Vision Plan for Rutgers University, *New Brunswick, New Jersey;* the Eyebeam Museum of Art and Technology Competition, *New York, New York;* BMW Central Building Factory Competition, *Leipzig Germany;* World Trade Center Design Competition, *New York, New York;* the European Central Bank Headquarters Competition, *Frankfurt am Main, Germany;* the Cincinnati Country Day School, *Cincinnati, Ohio;* the Korean Presbyterian Church of *New York, Sunnyside, Queens.*

RODOLFO MACHADO AND JORGE SILVETTI: graduate student housing for Harvard University, *Cambridge, Massachusetts;* a comprehensive master plan, a 267-bed dormitory, and a parking structure for Princeton University, *Princeton, New Jersey;* a museum for the University of Utah; a landmark tower for the University of Cincinnati in Ohio, *Cincinnati, Ohio;* the Wiess College dormitory and dining halls for Rice University, *Houston, Texas;* campus master plans for the University of California San Francisco, *San Francisco, California;* St. Albans School, Washington, DC; a branch of the Boston Public Library, *Massachusetts;* and Robert F. Wagner, Jr. Park, Battery Park City, *New York, New York.*

THOM MAYNE: Diamond Ranch High School, *Pomona, California;* Caltrans District 7 Headquarters, *Los Angeles, California;* the Eugene Federal Courthouse, *Eugene, Oregon* (2005); and the San Francisco Federal Building, *San Francisco, California.*

RICHARD MEIER: Atheneum, New Harmony, Indiana; The Hartford Seminary, *Hartford, Connecticut;* the High Museum of Art, *Atlanta, Georgia;* Frankfurt Museum for Decorative Arts, *Frankfurt, Germany;* the Canal Plus Television Headquarter, *Paris, France;* the Barcelona Museum of Contemporary Art, *Barcelona, Spain;* and The Getty Center, *Los Angeles, California.*

ERIC OWEN MOSS: Houses X and Y, *Malibu, California;* Lower East Side Housing/Indigent Pavilion *New York, New York;* The Box, *Culver City, California;* Contemporary Art Center and Theater, *Tours, France;* Gasometer D-1, *Vienna, Austria;* Beehive/Annex Conference Center, *Culver City, California;* Trvida, *Culver City, California;* Jewish Museum San Francisco, *San Francisco, California;* Dusseldorf Harbor, *Dusseldorf, Germany;* Green Umbrella; Arnoff Estate, *Calabassas, California;* Auschwitz Memorial and Museum, *Germany;* Oslo Opera House, *Oslo, Norway;* Stealth, Culver City, California; Queens Museum of Art, *Queens, New York;* and the Mariinsky and New Holland Cultural Center, *St. Petersburg, Russia.*

ENRIQUE NORTEN: National School of Theater at the National Center of the Arts, Churubusco, *Mexico City, Mexico;* the French Institute of Mexico, *Mexico City, Mexico;* the Museum of Natural History, *Mexico City, Mexico;* Televisa Mixed Use Building, *Mexico City, Mexico;* Televisa Dinning Hall, San Angel, *Mexico City, Mexico;* House LE, Colonia Condesa, *Mexico City;* Hotel Habita; The Jaguar Dealership, Santa Fé, *Mexico City, Mexico;* Princeton Parking Garage Structure, *Princeton, New Jersey;* Amsterdam Housing Building and Parque España Housing Building, Colonia Condesa, *Mexico City, Mexico.*

JEAN NOUVEL: Arab World Institute, *Paris, France;* the Tours Conference Center;, *Tours, France;* Opera House, *Lyon, France;* the Cartier Foundation Foundation headquarters, *Paris, France;* the Galéries Lafayette department store, *Berlin, Germany;* the Musée de la Publicite, *Paris, France;* the Museum of Contemporary Art, *Rome, Italy;* and the Lucerne Culture and Congress Center (2000).

WILLIAM PEDERSEN: Station Center, *White Plains, New York;* Westendstrasse 1/DG Bank Headquarters, *Frankfurt, Germany;* Rockefeller Plaza West, *New York, New York;* The World Bank, Washington, D.C.; Samsung Rodin Museum, *Seoul, Korea;* The Carwill House, *Stratton, Vermont;* 311 South Wacker Drive, *Chicago, Illinois;* Federal Reserve Bank, *Dallas, Texas;* 1250 Boulevard René Levésque/IBM Canadian HQ, *Montréal, Canada;* Capital Cities/ABC Headquarters, *New York, New York;* Shanghai World Financial Center, *Shanghai, China;* and the Buffalo Niagara International Airport, *New York*

I.M. PEI: Luce Memorial Chapel, *Taichung, Taiwan;* National Center for Atmospheric Research, *Boulder, Colorado;* National Gallery of Art, East Building, *Washington, D.C.;* John Fitzgerald Kennedy Library, *Boston, Massachusetts;* Bank of China Tower, *Hong Kong, China;* Grand Louvre, *Paris, France;* Four

CESAR PELLI: San Bernadino City Hall, *San Bernadino, California;* Pacific Design Center, *Los Angeles, California;* the United States Embassy, *Tokyo, Japan;* the Museum of Modern Art Expansion and Renovation, *New York, New York;* the World Financial Center, *New York, New York;* Canary Wharf Tower and Docklands Light Railway, *London, England;* North Carolina Blumenthal Performing Arts Center, *Charlotte, North Carolina;* Arnoff Center for the Arts, *Cincinnati, Ohio;* and Petronas Towers and Dewan Filharmonik Hallin *Kuala Lampur.*

RENZO PIANO: Centre Georges Pompidou, *Paris, France;* Prometeo Musical Space *Venice* and *Milan, Italy;* The Menil Collection Museum, *Houston, Texas;* S. Nicola Football Stadium, *Bari, Italy;* "Crown Princess" and "Regal Princess" cruise ships, Monfalcone, *Gorizia, Italy;* Kansai International Airport Terminal, *Osaka, Japan;* Cy Twombly Pavilion, *Houston, Texas;* Meriden hotel at *Lingotto* and Business Center, *Turin, Italy;* Ushibuka Bridge, *Kumamoto, Japan;* Atelier Brancusi, *Paris, France;* The Debis Building: Headquarters of Daimler Benz, *Potsdamer Platz, Berlin, Germany;* Daimler Benz Potsdamer Platz projects: musical theater, Imax theater, residentials, retails, *Berlin, Germany;* Lodi Bank Headquarters, *Lodi, Italy;* B1 Office Tower, Potsdamer Platz, *Berlin, Germany;* KPN Telecom Office Tower, *Rotterdam, The Netherlands;* The Giovanni and Marella Agnelli Art Gallery at *Lingotto, Turin, Italy;* and the Nasher Sculpture Center, *Dallas, Texas.*

CHRISTIAN DE PORTZAMPARC: Water tower, *Marne-la-Vallée, France;* Hautes Formes housing complex, *Paris, France;* Erik Satie Foyer Elderly Housing, *Paris, France;* Erik Satie Conservatory of Music, *Paris, France;* Elderly housing Château-des-Rentiers, *Paris, France;* Café Beaubourg, *Paris, France;* Dance School for the Paris Opera, *Nanterre, France;* Boutique Ungaro: *Paris, Humbourg, Hong-Kong, London, Los Angeles, Tokyo, Taipei, Zurich;* Extension of the Bourdelle Museum, *Paris, France;* Fukuoka housing complex, *Island of Kyushu, Japan;* Offices and Hotel Holiday Inn, *Paris, France;* Parc de Bercy housing complex, *Paris, France;* City of Music, Parc de la Villette *Paris, France;* Crédit Lyonnais Bank Tower, *Lille, France;* the Place Nationale transformation of housing complex, *Paris, France;* Canal + Office Complex, *Boulogne Paris, France;* L.V.M.H. Tower, *New York, New York;* Court of Justice, *Grasse, France;* Extension of the Parisian Convention Center, *Paris Porte Maillot, France;* and the French Embassy, *Berlin, Germany.*

ANTOINE PREDOCK: Museum of Albuquerque, *Albuquerque,* New Mexico the Rio Grande Nature Center master Plan & Visitor Center, *Albuquerque, New Mexico;* the Nelso Fine Arts Center at the Arizona State University in Tempe, *Arizona;* Venice House, *Venice, California;* Mandell Weiss Forum Theater at the University of California, *San Diego, California;* American Heritage Center & Art Museum at the Univesity of Wyoming in Laramie; Turtle Creek House, *Dallas, Texas;* Thousand Oaks Civic Arts Plaza, *Thousand Oaks, California;* Spencer Theater for the Performing Arts, *Alto, New Mexico;* Tang Teaching Museum and Art Gallery, Skidmore College, *Saratoga Springs, New York;* Shadow House, *La Tierra Nueva, New Mexico;* and Robert Hoag Raylings Library, *Pueblo, Colorado.*

WOLF PRIX: Rooftop Remodeling Falkerstrabe, *Vienna, Austria;* the masterplan for the city of *Melun-Sénart, France;* the Groniger Museum, the East Pavilion, *Gronigen, The Netherlands;* the UFA-Cinema Center, *Dresden, Germany;* the SEG Apartment Tower, *Vienna, Austria;* the SEG Apartment Block, *Vienna, Austria;* and the Apartment Building Gasometer B.

LORD ROGERS: Centre Culturel d'Art Georges Popidou, *Paris, France;* Lloyd's of London, *London, England;* Fleetguard, *Brittany, France;* National Gallery Extension, *London, England;* Thames Wharf Studios Complex, *London, England;* Royal Albert Dock Development, *London, England;* Marseille Airport, *France;* Terminal 5, *Heathrow, London;* Channel 4 Headquarters, *London, England;* Potsdamer Platz, *Berlin, Germany;* Shanghai Lu Jia Zui, *Shanghai, China;* Seoul Broadcasting Center, *Seoul, Korea;* Zurich Airport, *Zurich, Switzerland;* New Millenium Experience, *London, England;* Nippon Television Center, *Tokyo, Japan;* and Barajas Airport, *Madrid, Spain.*

LINDY ROY: E-Bar in the Grace Building, *New York, New York;* Moss Loft, *New York, New York;* Okavango Delta Spa, Botswana; Voucher House, *Houston, Texas;* El Valle Eco-Resort and Spa, *El Valle, Panama;* Poolhouse, *Sagaponac, New York;* Wind River Lodge, *Alaska;* Vitra, *New York, New York;* and Hotel 45, *New York, New York.*

SANAA: Multimedia Workshop, Gifu, Japan; S-House, *Okayama, Japan;* N-Museum, *Wakayama, Japan;* M-House, *Tokyo, Japan;* K-Building, *Ibaraki, Japan;* Koga Park Café, *Ibaraki, Japan;* O-Museum, *Nagano, Japan;* Day Care Center, *Kanagawa, Japan;* La Biennale di Venezia, 7th International Architecture Exhibition"City of girls" Japanese Pavilion, Exhibition Design, Arsenale, *Venice, Italy;* and Garden Cafe at the 7th International Istanbul Biennale, *Istanbul, Turkey.*

SHoP: Museum of Modern Art and P.S. 1 Contemporary Art Center "Dunescape" Summer Courtyard Installation, *Long Island City, New York;* Rector Street Bridge, *New York, New York;* The Porter House, *New York, New York;* Mitchell Park Village of Greenport, *Greenport, New York;* and the Virgin Atlantic First Class Lounge at JFK Airport, *New York, New York .*

ROBERT A.M. STERN: Norman Rockwell Museum, *Stockbridge, Massachusetts;* Feature Animation Building for the Walt Disney Company, *Burbank, California;* the Spangler Campus Center at the Harvard Business School, *Boston, Massachusetts;* the Nashville Public Library, *Nashville, Tennessee;* and the Hobby Center for the Performing Arts in *Houston, Texas.*

BERNARD TSCHUMI: Parc de la Villette, *Paris, France;* Le Fresnoy National Studio for Contemporary Arts in *Tourcoing, France;* Columbia University's Lerner Hall Student Center, *New York, New York;* the Interface Flon, a bus, train, and subway station and pedestrian bridge in *Lausanne, Switzerland;* Concert Hall and Exhibition Complex in *Rouen, France* (2001); and Florida International University School of Architecture in *Miami, Florida*

ROBERT VENTURI AND DENISE SCOTT BROWN: Sainsbury Wing of the National Gallery, *London, England;* the Seattle Art Museum, *Seattle, Washington;* the Museum of Contemporary Art, *San Diego, California;* the Mielparque Nikko Kirifuri Resort near Nikko, *Japan;* the French Départment de la Haute-Garonne Provincial Capital building, *Toulouse, France;* University of Pennsylvania's Perelman Quadrangle, *Philadelphia Pennsylvania;* Princeton University's Frist Campus Center, *Princeton, New Jersey;* the Baker/Berry Library at Dartmouth College, *Hanover, New Hampshire;* and the Anlyan Center for Medical Research and Education at Yale University, *New Haven, Connecticut.*

RAFAEL VIÑOLY: John Jay College of Criminal, *New York, New York;* the Tokyo International Forum, *Tokyo, Japan;* the Kimmel Center for the Performing Arts in *Philadelphia, Pennsylvania;* Watson Institute for International Studies at Brown University, *Providence, Rhode Island;* the University of Chicago Graduate School of Business, *Chicago, Illinois;* the University of California at Los Angeles Nanosystems Research Institute, *Los Angeles, California;* the Tampa Museum of Art, Tampa, Florida; the Nasher Museum at Duke University, *Durham, North Carolina;* the Howard Hughes Medical Institute Janelia Farm Research Campus, *Leesburg, Virginia;* and the Cleveland Museum of Art, *Cleveland, Ohio*

TOD WILLIAMS AND BILLIE TSIEN: Feinberg Hall, Princeton University, *Princeton, New Jersey;* New College, the University of Virginia, *Charlottesville, Virginia;* The Neurosciences Institute, *La Jolla, California;* The Phoenix Art Museum, *Phoenix, Arizona;* Long Island Residence, *Southhampton, New York;* The Cranbrook Natatorium, *Bloomfield Hills, Michigan;* The Mattin Art Center, John's Hopkins University, *Baltimore, Maryland;* and The Museum of American Folk Art, *New York, New York*

PETER ZUMTHOR: Atelier Zumthor, Haldenstein, *Graubünden, Switzerland;* Saint Benedict Chapel, Sumvitg, *Graubünden, Switzerland;* Art Museum Chur, *Graubünden, Switzerland;* Residential home for the elderly, Masans, Chur, *Graubünden, Switzerland;* Thermal Bath Vals, Vals, *Graubünden, Switzerland;* Art Museum Bregenz, Bregenz, *Vorarlberg, Austria;* Topography of Terror, International Exhhibition and Documentation Centre, *Berlin, Germany;* Swiss Pavillion EXPO 2000, *Hannover, Germany;* Villa in Küsnacht am *Zürichsee Küsnacht, Switzerland;* Laban Centre for Movement and Dance, *London, England;* Lichtforum Zumtobel Staff, *Zurich, Switzerland* (1997); and the Cloud Rock Wilderness Lodge Moab.

COPYRIGHTS (DRAWINGS)

ACKNOWLEDGMENTS

This project has provided me with so many rewards; I have met so many people who have inspired me as a person. The results of that inspiration, I hope, are reflected in my work. I found myself continuously trying to achieve a higher level of work to please those who have participated in this project.

I cannot simply acknowledge one or two of the architects. So many have generously provided me with introductions into their world—with ideas about what architecture means and how it works; I am eternally grateful.

The book might not have come to fruition without the forward thinking of Martine Assouline and her embracing of my work and the idea for this project. I also want to thank Prosper Assouline for his counsel and creative input.

So many people have come to my aid with guidance and support—the list is endless. I most especially want to thank the team at Assouline New York, which has been superb in helping to make the book flawless:

Karen Lehrman, editorial director, for her tireless devotion to the idea of the book and her continuous efforts to develop and finesse its strengths; Sarah Stein, assistant editor, for her patience with me, her subtle but outstanding suggestions, and her efforts at gathering all the materials; Ausbert de Arce, marketing director, for guiding me through this complex world of publishing; and Martin Lavoie, production manager, for helping me to put the final touches on the photographs so that they are fully realized.

Finally, a profound thanks to my family, to my better half, Barbara, to the support of Ken Gemes, and to all my new friends in this world because of this great journey…I am indebted for life.